St Andrews Street Names

Their origin and meaning

Robert N Smart and Kenneth C Fraser

St Andrews University Library
1995

Published by St Andrews University Library,
North Street, St Andrews, KY16 9TR

British Library Cataloguing-in-Publication Data
A cataloguing record for this book is available from the
British Library

ISBN 0 900897 13 9

Printed from CRC by Quick Print, St Andrews

St Andrews University Library gratefully acknowledge
financial assistance from St Andrews Common Good Fund
by courtesy of North-East Fife District Council, and the
permission of St Andrews Merchants' Association for the use
of the street plan of the town.

Introduction

THE EARLY STREET NAMES OF ST ANDREWS, so far as can be determined, are all descriptive and arise from popular use. This situation existed until the nineteenth century when the Town Council took responsibility. On 10 November, 1843 the Council agreed to a verbal request from the inhabitants of East Burn Wynd to change the name to Abbey Street, and a committee was appointed consisting of Baillie Robert Pattullo (the last of the Pattullos of Balhouffie), Peter Steele and David Bruce with power to carry out similar changes. What these were, altering Wynds to Streets and Lanes and anglicizing other Scotticisms, will be found detailed under the individual names. However national legislation was about to change the process of naming streets. The first and second burgh police acts (Burgh Police (Scotland) Act, 1833 and Police of Towns (Scotland) Act, 1850,) laid a duty on the Police Commissioners appointed under them to see that name-plates were put up on streets. The third act (General Police and Improvement (Scotland) Act, 1862) stated that no name should be given to any street without the consent of the commissioners, but the fourth act (Burgh Police (Scotland) Act, 1892) was couched in much stronger terms, saying that no name should be given to any street except by the Commissioners or with their consent. In practice the names of the nineteenth century tended to be chosen by the developers and often commemorated themselves or their family connections, while those chosen by the Commissioners tended to honour public figures. The Town Councils (Scotland) Act, 1900 transferred the powers of the Police Commissioners to the Town Council, who, for the next seventy-five years, became responsible for naming streets, sometimes fiercely jealous of their privilege, but occasionally prepared to accept the suggestions of interested parties like developers, builders or feudal superiors.

Until the First World War the naming pattern continued to follow that of the nineteenth century. It is notable that the streets formed on the University's land at Rathelpie were all named after figures from its history.

The Housing, Town Planning, etc. (Scotland) Act of 1919 enjoined local authorities to provide "working class houses", and St Andrews was an enthusiastic participant. Most of the new streets built for this purpose until 1950 were given the names of Provosts or Councillors, usually while they were still serving, but Chamberlain Street, King Street and later Churchill Crescent represented rare excursions into national politics. Private developments generally received names from the land they were built on, as did a few streets of council houses.

Tom Morris Drive, in 1951, brought in a new fashion of naming streets in the council housing schemes after golfers: this continued into the 1970's. As before, private developments usually received land-based names. In 1955, after several attempts, a scheme was agreed to rationalise the names of the many short terraces in the Old Town. To placate fierce local opposition the result was usually a compromise in which the names of both the terrace and the street were employed.

In the last years of St Andrews Town Council, efforts were made to name streets after almost every Provost since World War I who had not previously been so honoured: for the first time, such names were given to private developments but land-based names also continued in areas of private and municipal housing, and names of several historical characters were used as well.

The Local Government (Scotland) Act, 1973, which set up North-East Fife District Council in 1975, made little difference to the naming pattern. Since then, land-based names have continued to be frequent, the rest being mainly those of historical characters — to which have been added, in the 1990's, writers with local associations – or of people associated with the sites on which the developments took place. The cumbersome fashion of double-barrelled names has also continued. In recent years, though the recommendation of the local member of the District Council has usually been accepted, in practice Councillors have often put forward names suggested by the Community Council.

As yet another reform of local government takes place, it is to be hoped that the new authority will continue the good practice of its predecessors in rejecting the kind of stereotyped batches of names like Acacia Avenue which add to the monotony of so many new housing areas elsewhere, and instead choose names with genuine local associations in our historic city.

⸺ ❦ ⸺

WE HAVE INCLUDED in this publication some names within the burgh which are locations rather than streets in order that it may be a more complete guide to the topography of the town. Names with apostrophes caused us some difficulty (the usage is particularly haphazard, as indicated by the two name plates at either end of Crails Lane) and we have decided to leave them out as the elements in the placename have become disassociated from their original significance and now only 'mean' a geographical location.

The photographs have been chosen to complement the text. Each one portrays within it something which is no longer part of the view and demonstrates how much in the burgh has changed. The map on page 7 makes the point more particularly in relation to the growth of the built up area in relatively recent times.

This work is a continuation and amplification of that on the names of the old town of Dr Hay Fleming in the later editions of his Handbook and of Dr R G Cant in his work on the mediaeval and some of the later names first published in the St Andrews Preservation Trust Annual Report and Yearbook for 1964 and 1965. We have made free use of these. We are also indebted to the following individuals who have personally shared their knowledge with us and guided us to conclusions for which we alone are responsible: R G Cant, G Christie, E Eddie, C Forrest, D Gourlay, A H McKerrow, G McMillan, J C D Montgomery, D Niven, D D R Owen, G L Pride, J Reid, J Tynte and A N Warren.

The sources we have used in compiling this publication are very varied, from mediaeval charters to modern directories. However most of the information has been derived from three main origins; the minutes of official bodies (Town Council, Police Commissioners and District Council), stent and valuation rolls and newspapers. To have cited the authorities used for the individual entries would have extended this work to an impractical size, but it is believed that sufficient indications are given in most cases to enable further information to be obtained.

For the word processing, layout and design of this work we are entirely indebted to the cheerful industry of Nicola Marshall and Christine Wolfe.

List of Illustrations

Cover illustrations from slides by *Andrew Cowie*

Front: St Andrews from Kinkell Braes, 1975

Back: The Canongate, 1970

STREET PLAN

Legend

P	Parking		Built-up area
T	Toilets		Buildings of interest
+	Church		University buildings
GPO	General Post Office		Open spaces
PO	Sub-post Office		Tennis
18	Golf Course		Bowling
	Putting		Play Area
	Tourist Information Centre		

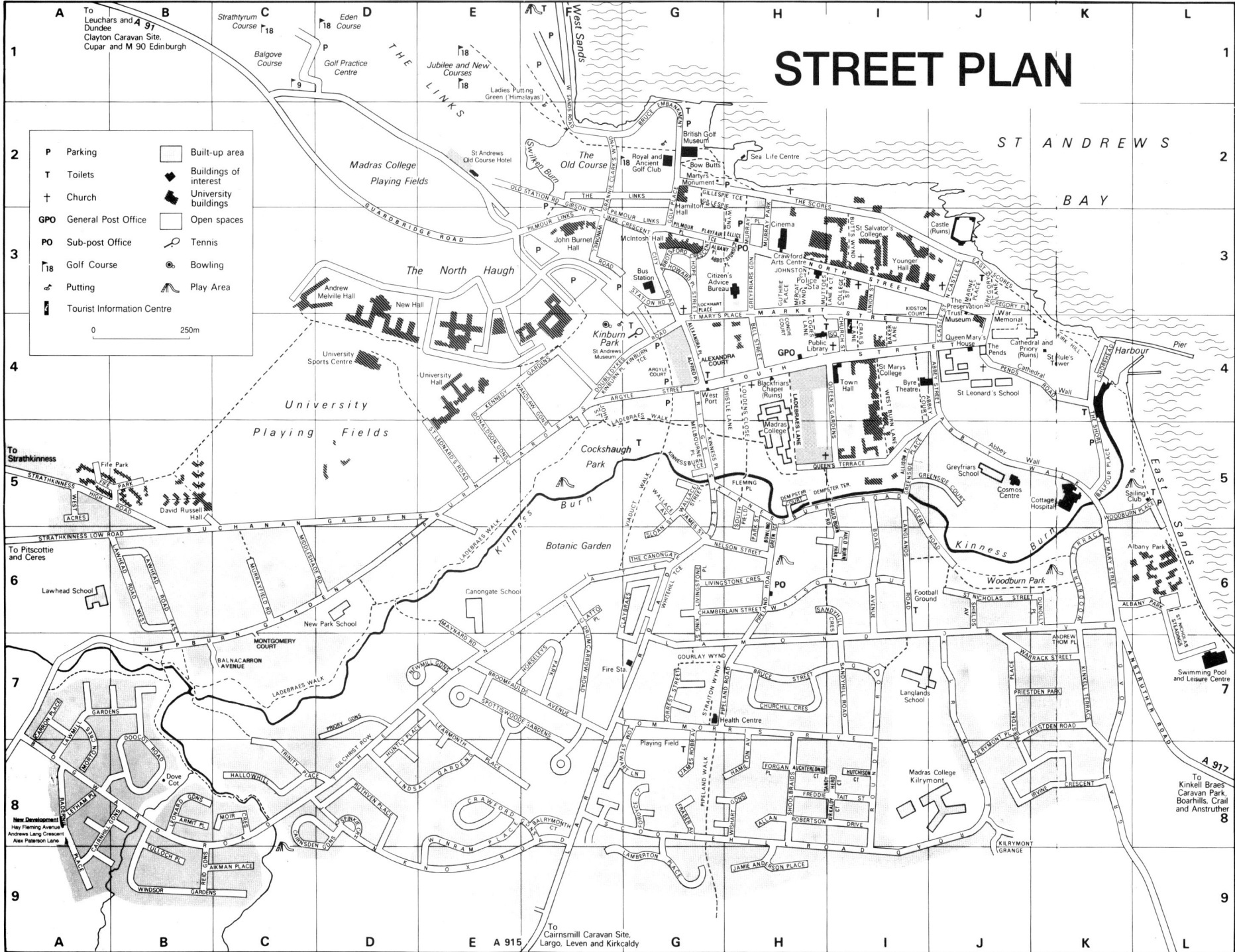

0 — 250m

ST ANDREWS BAY

To Leuchars and Dundee
Clayton Caravan Site,
Cupar and M 90 Edinburgh

A 91

To Strathkinness

To Pitscottie and Ceres

Strathkinness Low Road

New Development
Hay Fleming Avenue
Andrews Lang Crescent
Alex Paterson Lane

To Cairnsmill Caravan Site,
Largo, Leven and Kirkcaldy
A 915

To Kinkell Braes
Caravan Park,
Boarhills, Crail
and Anstruther
A 917

Golf Courses / Links
Strathtyrum Course
Eden Course
Balgove Course
Golf Practice Centre
Jubilee and New Courses
Ladies Putting Green ('Himalayas')
THE LINKS
The Old Course
West Sands
Swilken Burn
Bruce Embankment

Points of interest
Madras College Playing Fields
St Andrews Old Course Hotel
British Golf Museum
Royal and Ancient Golf Club
Sea Life Centre
Bow Butts
Martyrs Monument
The Scores
Hamilton Hall
Gillespie Tce
Gillespie
St Salvator's College
Castle (Ruins)
Cinema
Crawford Arts Centre
Police Sta
Younger Hall
The Preservation Trust Museum
War Memorial
The North Haugh
Madras College Playing Fields
John Burnet Hall
McIntosh Hall
Bus Station
Citizen's Advice Bureau
Andrew Melville Hall
New Hall
University Sports Centre
University Hall
Kinburn Park
St Andrews Museum
Kinburn
GPO
Public Library
Queen Mary's House
The Pends
Cathedral and Priory (Ruins)
St Rule's Tower
Cathedral
Harbour
Pier
Alexandra Court
Argyle Court
West Port
Town Hall
St Marys College
Byre Theatre
Blackfriars Chapel (Ruins)
Madras College
St Leonard's School
Queen's Gardens
Queen's Terrace
Cockshaugh Park
University Playing Fields
Fife Park
David Russell Hall
Botanic Garden
Greyfriars School
Cosmos Centre
Cottage Hospital
Sailing Club
Albany Park
Woodburn Park
Fire Sta
Canongate School
New Park School
Montgomery Court
Balnacarron Avenue
Lawhead School
Health Centre
Langlands School
Football Ground
Swimming Pool and Leisure Centre
Priestden Park
Madras College Kilrymont
Kilrymont Grange
Dove Cot
New Development
Kinness Burn

© Copyright St Andrews Merchants Association 1990

A B C D E F G H I J K L

1 2 3 4 5 6 7 8 9

KEY

Pre-1900
1900 – 1910
1910 – 1920
1920 – 1930
1930 – 1940
1940 – 1950
1950 – 1960
1960 – 1970
1970 – 1980
1980 – 1990
1990 –

0   500m

SCALE

N

THE DEVELOPMENT OF ST ANDREWS 1900 —

(Post 1900 developments within the pre 1900 area are omitted)

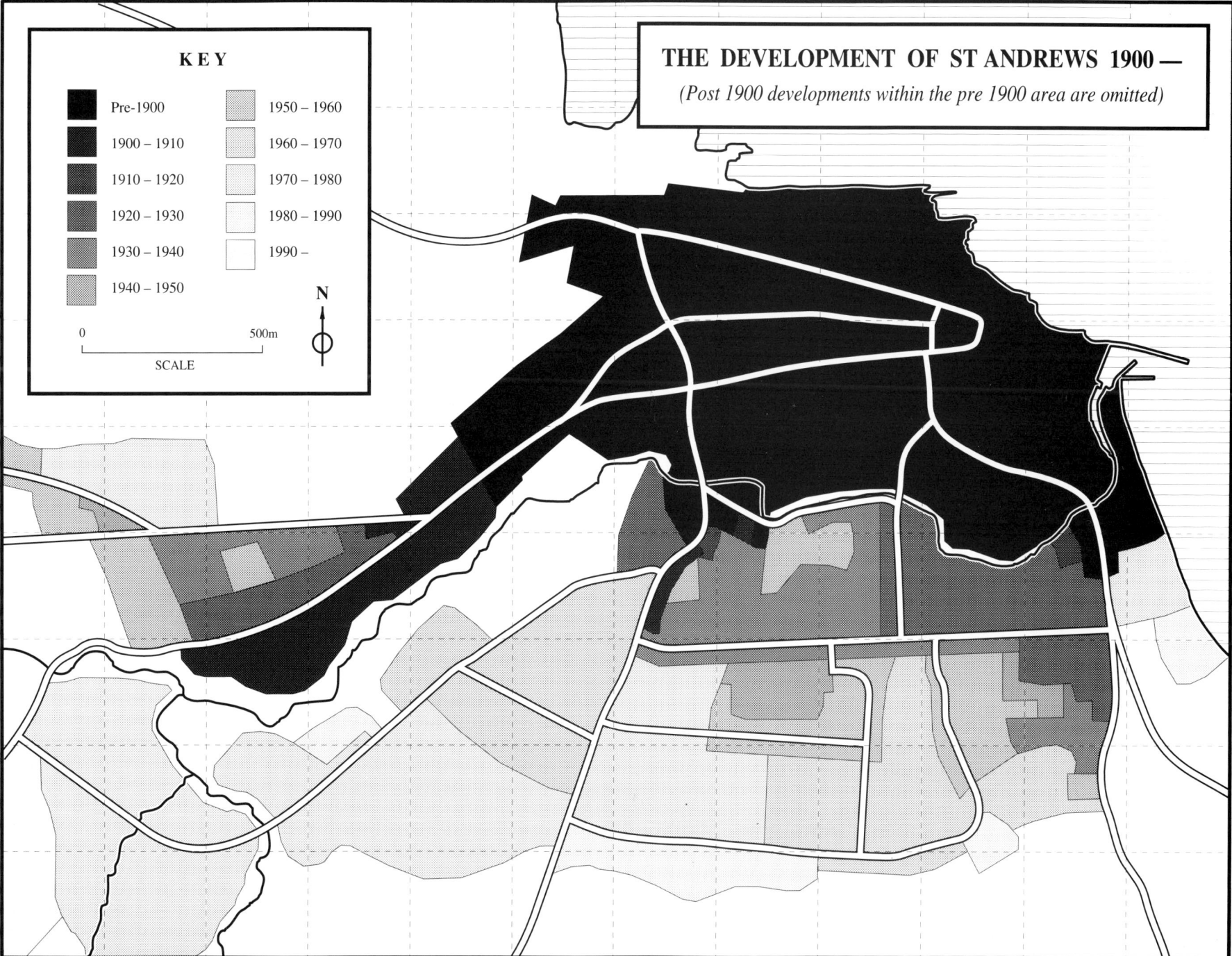

The keying squares in this map are similar to the Merchants Association map 1990, for ease of comparison.

3. *The old town hall in Market Street which was demolished in 1862. Although Sir Hugh Lyon Playfair is usually given credit for its replacement by the building in South Street, it was planned and the ground bought long before he became resident in the town. The outline of the old town hall can still be traced by the different coloured cobble stones let into the street.*

A

ABBEY CLOSE - located at the foot of the long rig pertaining to what is now 52 South Street. As an address for dwelling houses it existed from the mid-nineteenth century to just after 1900, then it continued as the location of a coach house, stables and store and is since 1956 once again the location of a house. [4I]

ABBEY COURT - Named c.1850 when houses were first developed on this site, based on the disused cornbarns, brewery and canvas factory, which had belonged to the entrepreneurial Dempster family. These houses were demolished in 1967 and the site was redeveloped for new houses. [4J]

ABBEY STREET - Originally known as Priors Wynd, the name became East Burn Wynd in the course of the sixteenth century. It was renamed Abbey Street, 10.11.1843 at the request of the inhabitants. [4J]

ABBEY WALK - The old continuation of East Burn Wynd south towards the crossing of the Kinness Burn, originally at Stermolind (=Gaelic *stair+muillean*, the crossing at the mill) later the Bow Brig. It was named Abbey Walk in 1843. No doubt the substitution of 'Abbey' for the correct 'Priory' in various street names at this time was under the influence of Colonel Andrew Glass naming the new house he built off this road about 1815, Abbey Park. [5J]

ABBOTSFORD CRESCENT - Built 1849-77 and named by the developer, James Hope, later Hope-Scott (1812-78) after the Border residence erected by Sir Walter Scott, who invented the name Abbotsford for it. For a short time it was named Gladstone Crescent after the first developer, Sir John Gladstone of Fasque (1764-1851), the father of the distinguished statesman, orator, scholar and writer, William Ewart Gladstone (1809-98), who bought the site in 1847. [3G]

ABBOTSFORD PLACE - Developed 1870 and took its name from the adjacent, but unconnected scheme of Abbotsford Crescent. It was originally intended to be called Abbotsford Square. [3H]

AIKMAN PLACE - Named 3.9.1973 after Provost Andrew Aikman (1846-1932). Andrew Aikman was partner and later owner of the high class grocery business of Aikman and Terras at the west corner of South Street and Bell Street, which continued until 1981. He was a town councillor 1877-98 and 1915-18, during which last period he was Provost. [9C]

ALBANY PARK - Developed 1973-74 as a University residence, it was given the name of one of the original four nations within the University, Albany comprehending students from Fife and part of Perthshire. This division of the students into four groups according to the geographical area of their birth-places was originally part of the government of the University and survived as a feature in the election of the Rector until 1858. [6L]

ALBANY PLACE - Named 9.4.1883 in honour of Leopold George Duncan Albert, Duke of Albany (1853-84), youngest son of Queen Victoria. In 1881 the ancient dukedom of Albany was revived in his favour, Prince Leopold was Captain of the Royal and Ancient Golf Club in 1876. Albany Place was previously known as Craig Place and North Street Road. [3G]

ALEX PATERSON LANE - Named 4.9.1991 in honour of Alexander B Paterson (1907-89) freelance journalist, author, playwright and founder member of the Byre Theatre. He was for more than forty years administrator of the Byre Theatre and was chairman of the theatre board. He was also chairman of the Federation of Scottish Theatres. [8A]

ALEXANDRA COURT - Named 3.7.1991 taking its name from the adjacent Alexandra Place. [4G]

ALEXANDRA PLACE - Developed 1869-70 and named after Alexandra, Princess of Wales (1844-1925), later Queen (1901-10), as wife of King Edward VII. She was the eldest daughter of Christian IX of Denmark and his wife, Louise of Hesse-Kassel and married Albert Edward, Prince of Wales in 1863. [4G]

ALFRED PLACE - Developed 1862-1870 and named after Prince Alfred Ernest Albert, Duke of Edinburgh and Duke of Saxe Coburg and Gotha (1844-1900) second son of Queen Victoria. In 1893 he succeeded his uncle, Ernest II, as Duke of Saxe Coburg and Gotha. He visited St Andrews in the 1860's when he was photographed by Thomas Rodger. [4G]

ALISON PLACE - Named 12.9.1898 on the application of the developer, Captain Robert Wilson, presumably after his wife Alison Wilson. This name is sometimes mistakenly spelled with two 'l's. [5I]

ALISONS CLOSE - Derives its name from the Alison family who had property here from at least 1784 until after 1834 when Catherine (Kitty) Alison had the property confirmed to her. She was still owner in 1840. [4H]

ALLAN ROBERTSON DRIVE - Named 13.2.1967 after Allan Robertson (1815-59), the first professional golfer in the world, who died unbeaten in a full match. The first Open Championship in 1860 was held to fill the gap caused by his death. [8H]

ANDREW LANG CRESCENT - Named 4.9.1991 in honour of Andrew Lang (1844-1912) classical scholar, journalist, anthropologist, poet, historian, miscellaneous writer and in a St Andrews context, student, Gifford lecturer and frequent visitor. He wrote the poem which begins "St Andrews by the Northern Sea A haunted town it is to me! A little city worn and grey, The grey North Ocean girds it round ..." [8A]

ANDREW THOM PLACE - Named 7.4.1976 in honour of Andrew Thom (1900-69) who for 45 years was captain of the St. Andrews Boys Brigade. He was also for 16 years a town councillor, a magistrate for 7 years and served the community in many other ways. From 1956 he was owner of Livingstone, builders, St Andrews. [7K]

ANSTRUTHER ROAD - This is one of the long-standing names of the town, being descriptive of the road to the burgh on the south coast of Fife called Anstruther (Gaelic, Athernynstruther, *Ethernan* + *sruith* = the stream of Ethernan, a Celtic saint, who died in Pictland, 699 A.D.), but building did not begin along it until 1812, when it was constructed as a turnpike road. See St. Marys Street. [6J]

ARGYLE COURT - Developed 1985-88 on the site of the old Argyle Brewery, which was remarkable for its deep well and old vaults, reckoned to be two centuries old. Owned by D.S. Ireland in the nineteenth century it was sold in 1902 to John Wilson, who had made aerated water in the town since 1877. The official address is 25 Argyle Street. [4G]

ARGYLE STREET - Originally just "Argyle", this ancient settlement outside the early burgh boundary may have been of Scottish origin as distinct from the Pictish original settlement which about 1144 became the burgh. The origin of the name is probably Gaelic *Earra Ghaidheal* = the limit, the boundary or borderland of the Gael. It was later included in the royalty of the burgh as far as Palfrey Wynd (or Johnny Gib's Wynd) where John Street now stands. It long antedates and has no connection with the Campbell family. [4G]

ARMIT PLACE - Named 3.9.1973 in memory of the family of that

4. This is arguably the most important street junction in St Andrews with South Street leading east, Argyll Street leading west, City Road going north and Bridge Street going south, and the site of the main mediaeval entrance to the burgh. The West Port is still in substantially the same form as it was built in 1589 by Thomas Robertson, mason in Blebo. On the left, the gable end was remodelled by David Henry by the insertion of the present shop front in 1903. On the right, West Port House was demolished in 1969. Photograph dated 1860.

5. *This view of St Andrews from the West Sands was taken about 1870. The Scores buildings are new, stark and raw and many present day landmarks are absent. The Catholic Church (1884-5), the Bruce Embankment (1893) and the Grand Hotel (1894) are all to be built and the Royal and Ancient Club House is still in its original form.*

name and their contribution to civic life, but certainly referring in particular to Commander George Gilmour Armit (1888-1966) a veteran of two world wars, who was a town councillor for 14 years and Dean of Guild for seven years. [8B]

AUCHTERLONIE COURT - Named 9.9.1963 in general recognition of the contribution of many members of the family to the game of golf, but as it was named virtually on the first anniversary of the death of Tom Auchterlonie, one of the well-known golf club manufacturers, he was perhaps particularly in mind. [8H]

AULD BURN PARK - Named 18.7.1955 and built on the part of the Priory Acres, extending to about 32 acres, acquired by St. Andrews Town Council in 1931 called Auld Burns or alternatively Short Langlands. The lands were bounded on one side by Pipeland Burn and on the north by Kinness Burn and may derive their name from this fact. Part of this land was set aside as a public playground. [6I]

AULD BURN ROAD - Named 8.5.1934 as an intended development of private feus. The remarks under Auld Burn Park also apply. There was a house and steading on the Auld Burn Park lands when they were acquired by the Town Council. [5I]

B

BAKER LANE - The oldest, fifteenth century, form is Baxter Wynd. In the sixteenth and seventeenth century this form alternated with Bakehouse Wynd. In the eighteenth century the name became Bakers Wynd and in 1843 this was altered to Baker Lane. [4I]

BALFOUR PLACE - Takes its name from the architect, Robert Balfour (1770-1867), who built his own dwelling here, the offices of which were later developed as separate houses. [5K]

BALNACARRON AVENUE - Named 2.3.1988, taking its name from Balnacarron, the house in whose grounds it was developed. Balnacarron was built in 1895 and was probably named from the nearby 'Carron' (q.v.) with a bit of antiquarian Celticism attached to give the pseudo-Gaelic Bal+na+carron = farm/settlement of the stony place. [7C]

BALRYMONTH COURT - Named 5.4.1978 after the farm lying about one mile due south. Gaelic Bal+righ+monadh = farm/settlement of the king's hill. [8F]

BASSAGUARD - The early forms of this name usually spell it Bassagart and sometimes Basaker. This appears to derive from Gaelic Bal+saggart = the farm of the priest. The form Basaker develops improbably into Bess Acre. The original area between the Kinnessburn and the Canongate extended to 52.5 acres and was also called Gaupyshade. The University developed 25 acres of it as a botanical garden from 1963. This is now run by North East Fife District Council. Development of the part to the east of the old railway line began in 1898 (see Wallace Street, James Street). Gaupyshade is simply the piece of land which gapes, but whether the gaping related to the lie of the land or a characteristic of the soil we do not know (See Middleshade). [5G]

BELL STREET - Developed 1847-86 as South Bell Street, it was decreed to be called Bell Street on 13.1.1896 when North Bell Street changed its name to Greyfriars Garden. The name honours the St Andrean, Andrew Bell (1753-1832), who created the Madras or monitorial system of education, where the older pupils play a part in teaching the younger. He left most of his considerable fortune for educational purposes and the senior school in St Andrews, the Madras College, remains as one of his chief benefactions. [4H]

BOASE AVENUE - Named 13.6.1932 (first houses completed June 1933) in honour of William Norman Boase (1870-1938), Provost of the town 1927-36, having first entered the council in 1919. Provost Boase worked in his father's company, Boase Spinning Co., Dundee, and for a long time before his death he was Chairman. He was also Captain of the Royal and Ancient Golf Club. [6I]

BOGWARD ROAD - Construction as a main distributor road linking with the Canongate was agreed 22.4.1968. It takes its name from the area of the Priory Acres over which it is built. The original extent of Bogward was slightly over 30 acres. The name is probably just descriptive of the one time undrained nature of the soil and is found elsewhere in Scotland, e.g. there was a Bog-ward alias Mekill-ward outside Kilwinning. The 'ward' element signifies an enclosed piece of land. [8A]

BOW BRIDGE - This name commemorates the mediaeval hump back bridge, which replaced the inconvenient tidal ford which in earlier times existed where Shore Bridge is now. The original bridge was swept away in a flood in August 1663 and temporarily replaced by a timber bridge. The eventual stone replacement slightly downstream of its original site has been modified on a number of occasions. [5K]

BOWLING GREEN TERRACE - Building of this street was begun in 1899 by William Peddie Stratton and it was first known as Peddie Buildings. The name was changed between December 1906 and September 1907 to incorporate the name of the adjacent bowling green, which was laid out in 1887. [6H]

BRIDGE STREET - This street had at least five older names. In the fifteenth century it was called the Water Wynd; in the sixteenth, the Ford Wynd; in the seventeenth the Corn Wynd; in the eighteenth century it was called the Well Wynd with Maggie Murrays Wynd as a colloquial alternative. It became Bridge Street in the renaming of November 1843. On 19.9.1906 the extension from Maggie Murrays Bridge to Wallace Street was decreed to be South Bridge Street. [5G]

BROOMFAULDS AVENUE - Named 1965, taking its name from that part of the Priory Acres on which it is built. The name originally applied to an area of approximately 25 acres and most obviously derives from the fact that at one time there were enclosures here, where there was broom growing. [7E]

BRUCE EMBANKMENT - Dates from August 1893 when George Bruce (1825-1904) started to reclaim this area from the sea by forming a barricade of four old fishing boats filled with stones on the seaward side. George Bruce was a cabinet-maker by profession, but was also a notable actor, poet, naturalist, town councillor, property owner and many other things beside. His "Wrecks and Reminiscences of St Andrews Bay", 1884, is of great value to historians. [2G]

BRUCE STREET - Named 26.4.1948 in honour of George Bruce (1882-1963), who came here as gas manager in 1918. He served thirty-five years in public life, during which he was Provost for two terms, 1942-48, and Convener of Fife County Council for two terms. [7H]

BUCHANAN GARDENS - Named 8.4.1901 on the recommendation

6. *View from the top of St Rule's tower looking west along South Street about 1878. This prospect dramatically demonstrates the small extent of the town at that time. The population was about six and a half thousand, but of the 2054 families within the parish, 427 lived in one room houses.*

7. *South Street in 1896 before the age of the motor car. The lime trees on the north side were planted in 1879 and those on the south side a year later. It was not the first attempt to beautify the streets with trees as the proprietor of Deans Court got permission in 1759 to plant the street outside his property. The magistrates cut these down in 1815 – and claimed the wood!*

of the University Court in honour of George Buchanan (1506-82), the greatest of Scotland's Latin poets and authors. He was Principal of St Leonard's College, St Andrews, 1566-70, and served as tutor to both Mary, Queen of Scots and James VI. His most notable work "De jure regni apud Scotos" was on the accountability of governors to the people they govern. [5D]

BURGHER CLOSE (behind 141 South Street) - Derives its name from the location of the second Burgher Kirk here, 1774-1826, having been previously in Imrie's Close. The Burgher Kirk was composed of those Seceders who were prepared to accept the oath whereby certain burgesses had to acknowledge 'the true religion within this realm'. The anti-burghers contended this implied a recognition of the established church. [4H]

BURNS WYND (Argyle Street) - This derives its name from the Burns family who long had property on the south side of Argyle Street to the west of this wynd, which is about half way along. [4G]

BUTTS WYND - Despite being part of the mediaeval town plan this road had no distinctive name until the seventeenth century when it became so called because it led to the Bow Butts where archery was practised at the west end of the Scores. The name survived an attempt in 1843 to replace it with Scores Lane and another in the 1850's to call it Butts Lane. [3I]

BYRE WYND - Named 9.3.1970, being the pedestrian way from South Court to Abbey Street. It takes its name from the Byre Theatre, which in turn took its name from the former byre or cowshed in which it was established in 1933. [4I]

C

CAIRNHILL GARDENS - Named 8.9.1969 after the farm called Cairnhill near Radernie, which because of its location in the Cameron reservoir catchment area was in the ownership of St Andrews Town Council. Cairnhill is a common farm name in many parts of Scotland. [8A]

CAIRNSDEN GARDENS - Named 18.12.1972 after the ancient small property of Cairns, of which Cairns Mill just to the south is now the only relic. The Gaelic carn = a heap of stones and a den is a narrow valley usually wooded, being in this case the valley of the Cairns Mill Burn which is adjacent to the street. [8C].

CANONGATE - The original development was named Canongate Road on 23.1.1922 (altered to Canongate on 3.2.1922) after the old road through the Priory Acres pertaining to the canons of the Augustinian Priory. The first extension was named 'The Canongate' on 29.4.1963. This caused confusion and it was decided 25.1.1989 that the whole street be called 'Canongate'. [6G]

CARRON PLACE - Named 8.9.1969 from Carron, a settlement on the Kinnessburn upstream of Lawmill. It is a frequent Scottish place name and is usually taken to denote a stoney river bank. [7A]

CATHEDRAL PLACE - A short-lived attempt to provide a distinctive address for Deans Court around the middle of the nineteenth century during the early years of the Stirling family ownership (1850-1931). [4J]

CHAMBERLAIN STREET - Named 17.10.1938 in honour of (Arthur) Neville Chamberlain (1869-1940), Prime Minister, 1937-40 whose policy of appeasement of Germany had just seemed to have met resounding success with the Munich Agreement of 30 September. [6H]

CHURCH SQUARE - The area between the rear of Holy Trinity Church and the back lands of the Market Street properties was originally part of the churchyard, but was encroached on by the building of the English School in 1811 and the town reservoir tank in 1819. The first now houses the public library (1961) and the latter was afterwards the fire station and is now public toilets. Other buildings were constructed later with frontages to Church Square. [4I]

CHURCH STREET - Previously called Kirk Wynd, presumably from 1411, when the parish church was relocated here from near the east end of the cathedral. The decision to rename it Church Street was taken 10.11.1843. [4I]

CHURCHILL CRESCENT - Named 26.4.1948 in honour of Winston Churchill (1874-1965), Prime Minister of Britain and Northern Ireland during the Second World War. [7H]

CITY PARK - The original house on the site was built by William Gibson of Duloch (1803-62) in 1851. His name is commemorated in the Gibson Hospital set up in accordance with his will. In 1979 plans were agreed to modify the house and build 22 flats in the grounds. Numbers were allocated on 5.9.1979 and the work was completed a year or two later. [4G]

CITY ROAD - The name dates only from 1843, but the road itself has existed since the Middle Ages. It was called the Cowgait in the fifteenth century as it led to the common pasture on the north west of the burgh. This became Cow Wynd in the sixteenth and seventeenth centuries. A name for the northern part was Windmill Path after the windmill, which stood on the high ground to the west of it. [3G]

CLATTO PLACE - Named 29.4.1963 after a settlement some four miles due west of St Andrews. While it has been suggested that the name derives from Gaelic *claddach* = a stony foreshore or river bank, the current wisdom regards it as of impenetrable derivation. [6F]

CLAYBRAES - Named 27.2.1961 after a small area, about ten acres of the Priory Acres lying between Largo Road, Kinnessburn Road and Pipeland Road. It is a name descriptive of the soil type. [6G]

COCKSHAUGH PARK - 'Cock' is a common initial element in Scottish place names but no forms of Cockshaugh earlier than the eighteenth century have yet been found and it is impossible to suggest which of the many explanations might apply. For the 'Haugh' part see North Haugh. This park was originally leased from the University in 1905 for twenty-five years by the burgh with the intention of turning it into a public park, and eventually in 1951 they bought the land. [5F]

COLLEGE STREET - In the fifteenth century this street was known as Mercat Wynd, then until about 1500 it was called Bucklar Wynd, thereafter College Wynd, St Salvators College (1450) having been established long enough to have become fixed as the most frequent destination of users of the street. [3I]

CONDIE COURT - Named December 1986 and built on the site of the former Condie cleek factory at 122 Market Street. About 1890 Robert Condie began cleek making here and soon established himself amongst the famous names who served the world market with golf clubs until the introduction of the steel shaft in 1929 and the mass production methods which accompanied it destroyed their trade. George Condie continued the business until about 1937. [4H]

COWPERS CLOSE - (at 166-168 South Street). Takes its name from the family, more usually spelt 'Coupar', who had property here for

8. *The match in progress on the eighteenth green shows two of the great golfers of the town who have both been commemorated in street names, Freddie Tait is putting and old Tom Morris is holding the flag. The rough and pitted surface of the green shows what a tremendous golfer Freddie Tait was. In 1890, his first year of membership of the R&A, he lowered the Old Course record to 77 and later to an incredible 72.*

9. *Hybrid oats, developed by Dr John Hardie Wilson, lecturer in agriculture, St Andrews University 1900-1920, growing on the East Langlands area of the Priory Acres in 1910. The Boys Brigade Hall, designed by Gillespie & Scott, architects, St Andrews in 1899, is the first building in the left distance, below the tower of St Salvator's College on the skyline.*

several generations and who could either have derived their name from their original occupation of barrel making or from their progenitor coming from Cupar in Fife. [4H]

CRAILS LANE - Rentals from properties here were shortly after 1517 assigned to the endowment of the Collegiate Church of Crail, but it seems to have been only in the eighteenth century that Crails Wynd replaced the older name of New Close and this was in turn changed in 1843 to Crails Lane. [4I]

CRAWFORD GARDENS - Named 18.12.1972 in honour of the Earls of Crawford, who in various ways have been associated with the locality and the burgh for many centuries. [8H]

CUNNINGYARD - Coningyard, Cuningar and various other spellings. From the Scots *cuningar* = a rabbit warren. This part of the Priory Acres measuring some 25 acres in the angle between the Kinness Burn and the Crail/Anstruther road was operated as its name suggests (*cunnicularium* in Latin documents) as a warren in the first half of the sixteenth century. In the course of that century it was converted to arable and was acquired by St Marys College in 1685. The College feued out part for building in 1812 (see St Marys Street) and in 1920 sold the remainder to St Andrews Town Council for housing. [6K]

D

DAUPHIN HILL - The earliest forms of this name are Dapon Hill, Dappin Hill, Daupin Hill. It is derived from the dapping process used by the washer women and dyers who frequented this area until the Town Council started feuing it out from 1776 onwards. The 'h' is a nineteenth century addition and the name has no connection with the eldest son of the King of France. [5J]

DEMPSTER BRAE - This is an old path from the lade to the Kinness burn which is listed on 3.4.1851 as one of the immemorial rights of way. The name Dempster became attached to it after the development of Dempster Terrace to which it leads. [5I]

DEMPSTER COURT - Named 29.5.1985 by influence of the nearly adjacent Dempster Terrace. [5I]

DEMPSTER TERRACE - Developed 1870-1901 and named after the Dempster family who for two generations at the end of the eighteenth and beginning of the nineteenth centuries represented the entrepreneurial spirit in St Andrews, owning a distillery and a canvas factory and being engaged in many other projects including raising rabbits on the Links. This last gave rise to litigation, which wasted their fortune. [5I]

DICKIEMANS WYND - See Gregory Lane.

DOCTORS DYKES - This old road was obliterated and superseded by the new streets in the Priestden Parks development, 1930. The name may have originated in the fact that the land immediately to the East belonged to St Marys College. [7K]

DONALDSON GARDENS - Named 14.1.1901 on the recommendation of the University Court in honour of Sir James Donaldson (1831-

1915), Principal of St Andrews University from 1886 until his death. He was made an honorary burgess of the town in 1912. [5E]

DOOCOT ROAD - Named 15.3.1971 overturning an earlier (8.9.1969) decision to call it Dovecot Road and taking its name from the nearby sixteenth century Priory doocot. [8B]

DOUBLEDYKES ROAD - The name can be traced to the eighteenth century, but the fifteenth century name was Aberdonnsy Gait later Dunses Dykes, probably derived from a structure known as Dunses Hall which was situated between it and Argyle Street. It was called Doubledykes because up to 1887 it was a long strip of grass with a dyke on either side. [4F]

DRUMCARROW ROAD - Named 29.4.1963 from the hill Drumcarrow some three and a half miles south west of St Andrews. The early form of the name is Drumcarachin which is usually explained as Gaelic drum = ridge+carrach = rough, but it may be a derivation of drum+caer = a fort, being a reference to the prehistoric fortified structure, which was erected on it. [7F]

DUNOLLY PLACE - Named 28.6.1926 after the cottage built by Dewar Lauder, farmer, St Nicholas on the southmost part of the Cunningyard, which he feued from St Marys College in 1879. The name is, for some unknown reason, almost certainly transferred from the fortified site of great antiquity near Oban. Dunollie is the "Fort of Onlach or Ollach son of Brión" of whom nothing else is known. [6K]

E

EAST SCORES - Named 14.1.1952 in connection with an extensive renumbering scheme for the burgh, but not fully implemented until 1955. Previously it had just been referred to as part of The Scores (q.v.). [3J]

EDDIE COURT - Named 4.3.1992 in memory of Robert Eddie (1909-86), joiner, South Street. The development is built on the site of the burgh fire station, 1933-1972, and Robert Eddie was station officer 1961-70 having served at the station for 24 years. In 1972 it was moved to Largo Road. [5G]

ELLICE PLACE - Named 9.4.1883 in memory of Edward Ellice (1810-80), M.P. for St Andrews Burghs, 1837-80. The houses comprised were previously known severally as North Street Road, Ritchie Place, Ellice Place, Kinnaird Cottage and Eden Cottage. [3H]

10. *The west side of Union Street in late 1933 or early 1934. In 1933 the St Andrews Town Council designated this area a slum clearance scheme and it was mostly demolished soon thereafter and the site acquired by the University in 1934. Various buildings were proposed for the site, including a new Physics Building, but eventually in October 1964 the Buchanan Arts Building was completed. During the war the National Fire Service had a large static water tank on the site and one house remained in use and occupation until 1962.*

11. *Part of the Jubilee procession in Langlands Road, 6 May, 1935. The town's fire engine was acquired in 1921 and cost £1,953. Its first working call was to a fire at Crawford Priory in June of that year. It covered the twelve mile journey in 20 minutes and had ten hoses operating within 10 minutes.*

F

FIFE PARK - Named 13.10.1971 by the University Court to mark the contribution made by Fife County Council to the costs of this University residential complex. [5A]

FLEMING PLACE - This site in the South Haugh with its old flax spinning mill (James Reid & Son) was purchased by John Fleming, china and stoneware merchant in 1849 and converted into the fourteen houses which bear his name. This John Fleming was father to David Hay Fleming (1849-1931), the St Andrews historian and antiquary. [5H]

FORDYCE COURT - Named 1.2.1978 in honour of Thomas Thomson Fordyce (1896-1989), Provost of St Andrews, 1961-70. One of a small band of North East men who enriched St Andrews life, T. T. Fordyce came to St Andrews in 1924, buying the drapery business of Greig in South Street and on that based an expanded business owning two shops in St Andrews, a shop in Cupar and his original shop in Methil. [8G]

FORGAN PLACE - Named 13.12.1967 in honour of Robert Forgan (1824-1900), founder of the famous golf club making firm of Robert Forgan and Sons which he took over from his uncle Hugh Philp in 1852. He built up a reputation in the quality end of the trade, employing 50 people at his death. The firm was taken over by Messrs Spalding, who closed the works on 31.3.1963. [8H]

FORREST STREET - Named 15.3.1971 as Forrest Road but immediately emerged as Forrest Street commemorating Henry Forrest, who was burned as a heretic at St Andrews, probably in 1533, although his main crime appears to have been the possession of a New Testament in English. He was from Linlithgow and graduated from St Leonards College in 1526. [7G]

FOUNDRY LANE - See GREGORYS LANE.

FRASER AVENUE - Named 28.8.1972 in memory of David Fraser (1879-1962), Provost 1955-58. The son of a Strathkinness quarry master, David Fraser was a town councillor from 1931-1958. He was also a County Councillor for over 20 years and as convener of the County Water Committee he opened the Glendevon reservoir in 1955. [8G]

FREDDIE TAIT STREET - Named 9.9.1963 after Frederick Guthrie Tait (1870-1900) one of the great amateur golfers of his period, winning the amateur championship in 1899. He was killed in the Boer War. About half the cost of the Cottage Hospital built in 1902 was met from the Freddie Tait memorial fund. [8H]

FROWIS WYND - While this name has puzzled previous writers it is probably an early (pre-1450) name for College Street (q.v.). Frow signifies a Dutch woman. It has been identified from its contiguity with the property of Henry Brand. [3I]

G

GIBSON PLACE - Developed 1859-71 on ground feued by James Gibson, wood merchant, St Andrews (1800-58) in 1843. [2F]

GILCHRIST ROW - Named 10.1.1979 after John Gilchrist (b.1903) the last Provost of St Andrews before the May 1975 reform of local government. It was the last street to be named after a living person. [8D]

GILLESPIE TERRACE - Developed 1849-54 and named after Thomas Gillespie (1778-1844), professor of humanity, 1835-44, who took a prominent part in local affairs and was the moving spirit behind the erection of the Martyrs Monument just opposite. [2G]

GILLESPIE WYND - Named 18.4.1955. Although it had existed as a lane connecting the Scores and North Street ever since the properties were developed, naming was now regarded as necessary as it led to a dwelling house erected on the back lands of one of the properties the lane served and to which it was the only access. [2G]

GLEBE ROAD - Named 28.12.1927. It was partially built on lands which belonged to the Kirk Session of St Andrews parish church (Holy Trinity). The land did not form part of the glebe, which lay adjacent to the north on the other side of Kinnessburn. The glebe was the land amounting to approximately four Scots acres arable, which heritors were bound to provide for the minister of the parish. [5I]

GOLF PLACE - Developed 1830-37. This name originally applied to one side of the street, the other side being called Kirk Place after the developer, but it was decided on 19.1.1907 that the name Golf Place should apply to the whole street. [3G]

GOURLAY WYND - Named 15.3.1971 in memory of Norman Gourlay (c. 1497-1534) who was martyred along with David Straiton (see Straiton Wynd) at the foot of Calton Hill in Edinburgh "after dinner on 27 August, 1534", being first hanged then burnt. Gourlay graduated from St Andrews University in 1515. [7G]

GRANGE ROAD - The road leading to what was originally a religious house's outlying grange or farm, where grain and teinds were stored. It is very ancient as there is a reference to the "new" grange in 1248. Sites along it began to be feued for building in 1928. [8K]

GRANNIE CLARKS WYND - Originally throughout the nineteenth century known as Clarks Wynd from the site on the south east corner being originally feued in 1820 to George Clark, butler to Patrick Playfair of Dalmarnock. The 'Grannie' element appears to have been added this century, but whether from a genuine folk memory or whether, as is alleged, from the fertile imagination of W. T. Linskill, is unknown. [2F]

GREENSIDE COURT - Named 17.4.1985 as a development off Greenside Place, q.v. [5J]

GREENSIDE PLACE - Developed from about 1815 and named because it was adjacent to an area long in use as drying greens. [5I]

GREGORY GREEN - A name in use until the 1920's for part of the broad eastern extremity of North Street which was partly in grass. It took its name from Thomas Gregory, shipmaster (fl. 1715x40) who used to store his timber imports here. [3J]

GREGORY PLACE - Like the foregoing Gregory Green it takes its name from Thomas Gregory, shipmaster, who had property here. [3J]

GREGORYS LANE - This street was part of the mediaeval town plan, but it lacked a distinctive name until comparatively late. In the

12. *Abbey Street dressed up for the Jubilee of George V celebrated on 6 May 1935. Incredibly almost the entire mediaeval street was swept away as recently as 1969/ 70 as part of a road widening scheme although it must be admitted that few of the individual buildings were of great age. At the end of the street, on South Street can be seen the premises of the Co-operative Society, which traded there from the beginning of the century until the nineteen seventies.*

13. Lamond Drive in 1935. One of the entirely new streets under the Housing, Town Planning etc. (Scotland) Act of 1919. The first phase was not part of a grand design to lay out a new street linking the Crail and Anstruther roads to the Largo Road and by this date it only extended as far as Boase Avenue.

sixteenth century it was sometimes called Baxter Wynd as the baxter trade had land on the east side of it. In the eighteenth century it came to be known as Dickiemans Wynd (= Wynd of the servant of Richard). Its present name derives, as with the two previous names, from the time when the Gregory family had property here. Sometimes referred to as Foundry Lane from William Blyth's St Andrews Foundry which was located at the seaward end c.1851-1920. [3J]

GREYFRIARS GARDEN - Laid out and built in 1835-44 and originally named North Bell Street, but on 13.1.1896 the name was changed to Greyfriars Garden following on a petition from the feuars. It is on the site occupied by the house of the Franciscan or Grey Friars founded in the fifteenth century, which came into the possession of the burgh in 1567. [3H]

GUARDBRIDGE ROAD - Obviously descriptive of the road to Guardbridge, an old crossing of the River Eden. The old bridge, which still exists, was originally built by Henry Wardlaw, Bishop of St Andrews, 1403-40. The name Guard Bridge is from the Gaelic *gobhar* = a goat. The current local pronunciation of Gairbrig is more appropriate to its etymology than the mistaken gentrification to Guardbridge. [3E]

GUTHRIE PLACE - A previously unnamed property on the north side of Market Street on the backlands of which James and John Farquharson, plumbers, built in 1860 a range of new houses. Guthrie was James Farquharson's mother's maiden name. [3H]

H

HALLOWHILL - Named 18.12.1972 after the area on which it is built, meaning the Holy or consecrated hill. An ancient graveyard was located here on which a major archaeological excavation was carried out in 1975-77. This hill may also be the site of Eglisnamin, the unlocated church in the vicinity of St Andrews, which is referred to about 1150. The acreage covered by Hallowhill in the Priory acres is 12.836. [8C]

HAMILTON AVENUE - Named 1.6.1970 in memory of Patrick Hamilton (c. 1504-1528), one of the first Protestant martyrs who was nephew to the Earl of Arran by his father and to the Duke of Albany by his mother. A disciple of Luther and Melancthon he was burned before the gate of St Salvators College on the spot which is still marked. [8H]

HAY FLEMING AVENUE - Named 4.9.1991 in memory of David Hay Fleming (1849-1931). A native of St Andrews, he succeeded to his father's business as a china merchant from which he retired at an early age to devote himself to historical research. The principal subjects of his many books were the Scottish Reformation and the history of St Andrews. He bequeathed his extensive library in trust to his home town. [8A]

HEPBURN GARDENS - Named 14.1.1901 on the recommendation of the University Court after John Hepburn (c. 1458-1525), Prior of St Andrews, 1482-1522, who founded St Leonards College in 1512 and was an unsuccessful candidate for the Archbishopric of St Andrews in 1514. His most imposing extant monument is the Priory wall, which bears his arms at nine different locations. Apart from an early farm, building began along this road in 1880. [5E]

HOPE STREET - Developed 1847-80 and named after the developer James' Hope (1812-73), third son of General Sir Alexander Hope of Rankeillour, and son-in-law of John Gibson Lockhart. James Hope assumed the name Scott to become Hope-Scott. He lived at Abbotsford from 1853 until his death. He was an extremely successful barrister and had, in addition to Abbotsford, a highland estate, a home in London and another in France. [3G]

HORSELEYS PARK - First suggested on 29.4.1963 and defined as Horseleys Park on 2.9.1963. The name is taken from that part of the Priory Acres on which it is built. The original area stretched from the Largo Road to the Canongate and measured about 32 acres. The name horse+leys = those areas of pasture set aside for the grazing of horses. [7F]

HOWARD PLACE - Developed 1864-98 and named after the developer James Hope's second wife, Lady Victoria Alexandrina Fitzalan-Howard (1840-70), daughter of the 14th Duke of Norfolk, whom he married in 1861. [3G]

HUCKSTER WYND - See South Castle Street.

HUNTLY PLACE - Named 18.12.1972 after two generations of George Gordons, 4th and 5th Earls of Huntly. The 4th took up arms against Queen Mary and was slain at the battle of Corrichie in 1562, the 5th was condemned for treason, but pardoned. [8D]

HUTCHISON COURT - Named 9.9.1963 after Jock Hutchison (1884-1977), the St Andrews born American winner of the 1921 Open championship at St Andrews. [8I]

I

IMRIES CLOSE - Takes its name from the Imrie family, brewers and land labourers, who had property here in the eighteenth century. It was in this close that from 1749-1774 the first Secession (Burgher) Kirk was sited in what was originally a barn, then a house, later renovated by St Andrews Preservation Trust. It is located at 136 South Street. [4H]

IRVINE CRESCENT - Named 23.6.1952 in honour of Sir James Colquhoun Irvine (1877-1952), Principal of St Andrews University, 1921-52. He was a distinguished chemist and his period of office was notable for a great expansion of the University, which feued this ground for houses for its staff. The University had proposed to call the street after Provost Tulloch, q.v. [8K]

J

JACOBS LADDER - This is a pathway of some antiquity but it is not found named until the second half of the nineteenth century. The reference is to the ladder seen by Jacob leading up to heaven (Gen. xxviii, 12), hence its application in many places to steep ladders and pathways. [3F]

JAMES ROBB AVENUE - Named 28.8.1972 in honour of James Robb (1878-1949), British Amateur golf champion, 1906. Educated at Madras College he was a banker in Ayr and Prestwick and retired to St Andrews in 1940. [8G]

JAMES STREET - Named 12.7.1898 on the recommendation of Bailie

14. *Loudens Close, South Street in 1936. As one of its first tasks St Andrews Preservation Trust purchased this Close in 1939 from the Louden family. In 1941 the first part was renovated and in 1949 the building fronting the street was preserved. The two later houses at the south end of the Close were sold under restrictive conditions for renovation. The outside toilets tacked on to the original buildings disappeared in the reconstruction.*

15. *The gates and lodge to the Priory house are seen at the extreme east end of South Street (see under Priory) and to the left is the Abbey Bookshop, run by J H Whyte between 1931 and 1938. Whyte supported many aspects of the Scottish cultural revival of the time, selling, publishing and holding art exhibitions.*

David Henry a St Andrews architect. The reason is uncertain, but it is probable that it was after the six Stuart kings of Scotland, who bore this name. The belief that it was named after the original building of the chapel of St James is incorrect as it was not transferred to the street as a roller skating rink until October, 1909. [5G]

JAMIE ANDERSON PLACE - Named 12.1.1982 in honour of James Anderson (1842-1905), Open Champion 1877, 1878 and 1879, winning at Musselburgh, Prestwick and St Andrews. Anderson was the second man to win three consecutive championships. [9H]

JOHN COUPAR COURT - Named 1.9.1993 after John Coupar (1797-1879), land labourer or farmer, Bridge Street, whose family owned the land on the west side of the street allegedly for 500 years. He was also the Cupar carrier and was a town councillor from 1853-57. His daughter married J. D. Spence who had his builders' yard on this site. [4G]

JOHN KNOX ROAD - Named 18.12.1972 after John Knox (c. 1514-72), the most eminent promoter of the Reformation in Scotland, who is believed to have had part of his education at St Andrews University. After his conversion he joined the Protestants occupying St Andrews Castle in 1546. Following his captivity for three years he spent much of the period until his return to Scotland in 1555 in England and Geneva. He was again in St Andrews in 1559 preaching his typically vigorous sermons which inspired the Reformers on to victory. [9E]

JOHN STREET - Developed 1869 by the builder John Burns and named after himself on the croft which of old was called Purroc and the road on its west side which is now the street was variously called Palfrey Wynd, Pamphery's Wynd and Purroc's Wynd. A 'purroc' or 'parrock' was simply an enclosed area perhaps in this case used for horses as the alternative name 'palfrey' might suggest. [4F]

JOHNSTON COURT - Named 4.2.1976 after the former owners of the site (Johnston Ltd.) on which it was developed. William Johnston (1854-1917) had a livery stable which developed into a garage. The premises latterly stretched all the way through from Market Street, but the North Street end was acquired after William Johnston's death. Mercat Wynd (q.v.) has been developed on the southern part of the site. [3H]

K

KATE KENNEDY COURT - This unofficial name was given by the developers to the block of flats which on 5.9.1990 was allocated numbers in James Street. Kate Kennedy, the mythical niece of the founder of St Salvators College, Bishop Kennedy, is commemorated by a historical pageant every spring by the students of St Andrews University. [6G]

KENNEDY GARDENS - Named 14.1.1901, on the recommendation of the University Court, in honour of James Kennedy (c. 1408-1465), Bishop of St Andrews 1441-1465, who in 1450 founded St Salvators College as a constituent college of the University of St Andrews. Kennedy took a leading role in national affairs. [4E]

KIDSTON COURT - Named 7.9.1983 in memory of Annabel Kidston (1896-1981), artist and art teacher. Trained at the Glasgow School of Art, she came to St Andrews in 1936 and the very next year she was one of the moving spirits in the creation of St Andrews Preservation Trust. She busied herself in the affairs of the Trust for the rest of her life, and lived latterly at 21 Market Street. [3I]

KILRYMONT CRESCENT - Named 31.5.1989 by association with

the adjacent Kilrymont Road q.v. [8J]

KILRYMONT PLACE - Named 1.12.1958 by association with the adjacent Kilrymont Road q.v. [8J]

KILRYMONT ROAD - Named 10.10.1955 using the Anglicised form of the Gaelic Cill Rimhinn = *cill+righ+beinn* = church of the king's hill. This, according to the Scotichronicon, was the name of the settlement from about the 4th-9th centuries A.D. before it was changed to St Andrews by Kenneth MacAlpin. It continues to be the Gaelic name. However, the ancient etymology may be more complicated as it is rendered in the Tigernach Annals as *Cenrigmonaid, Cindrigh monagh/monaidh* and in the Chronicle of the Picts, *Cell Cindrigmonaid.* [7J]

KINBURN PARK - The grounds of the mansion house, Kinburn which were acquired along with the house by St Andrews Town Council in 1920 and laid out for a variety of recreational purposes. The house has been put to several different uses, but since 1991 it has housed a local authority museum. The name Kinburn is said to derive from an anglicised version of the Russian forts , which were captured by the British Army during the Crimean War just about the time the house was constructed (1855-56). [4F]

KINBURN PLACE - Developed from 1863 by John & James Farquharson on ground feued from the properties of Kinburn House. [4F]

KINBURN TERRACE - Developed from 1869 for Robert Tullis and taking its name from the nearby Kinburn House. [4G]

KING STREET - Named 29.8.1938 after King George VI (1895-1952) who reigned 1937-52. The name reflects the patriotic feelings evoked by the danger of war, which was particularly acute at that date (see Chamberlain Street). [6G]

KINKELL TERRACE - Named 27.2.1928 and taking its name from the ancient property, which once had a castle, above the cliffs on the east side of the Crail road just outside St Andrews. Kinkell is explained as Gaelic *ceann+coille* = head of the wood. [7K]

KINNESSBURN GARDEN - Named 4.9.1991 after the adjacent burn. (See Kinness Place). [5G]

KINNESSBURN ROAD -Parts of this road were of old farm roads and it was extended eastwards from the late nineteenth century. However, in 1929 the link from Bowling Green Terrace to the Greenside Place Bridge was constructed and from then on it is known as Kinnessburn Road. It is not, however, until 1934-35 that it appears in the Valuation Roll as an address, the western part having previously appeared as Fleming Place Road. (See Kinness Place). [5H]

KINNESSBURN TERRACE - Developed and named 1895. (See Kinness Place). [5G]

KINNESS PARK - Developed and named about 1881 by Thomas Harris, joiner and building contractor. (See Kinness Place). The Kinness Park houses were allocated numbers in Kinnessburn Road in 1955. [5H]

KINNESS PLACE - Developed and named about 1873 although two of the houses are a year or two older. This is the earliest of the Kinness group of names, taking its name from the Kinness burn - the main stream flowing through St Andrews to the sea. The derivation seems to be Gaelic *ceann+eas* = the head stream, probably as delimiting the southern boundary of the town. The survival of a single early example of the spelling 'Kined' has suggested to some etymologists that it may be derived from the personal name Kenneth. [5G]

KIRKALDY COURT - Named 9.9.1963 in memory of Andrew

16. *Market Street from the junction with Greyfriars Gardens and Bell Street, in 1938. On the left hand side is Kermath's Pharmacy, an old established business which closed in 1970; Woolworths had recently opened its doors on 8 April 1936 as had Hepworths, the mens tailors (also 1936). Just beyond were three grocers next door to each other, Wm Low, the Maypole Dairy and John Currie. Immediately opposite was another grocer, Liptons. St Nicholas Dairy (1935) and Greenside Downes (1929), a branch of the Edinburgh George Street outfitters, are at this end on the south side.*

17. *The junction of Hepburn Gardens and Buchanan Gardens having in the background the entrance to Donaldson Gardens, marked by St Leonard's Church. Shows the Super de luxe 1901 model Panhard Levassor belonging to Dr James Younger of Mount Melville returning to St Andrews, having taken part in the Edinburgh to Glasgow 'Old Crocks' run in connection with the Empire Exhibition at Bellahouston Park. Tom Methven is the Mount Melville chauffeur. September, 1938.*

("Andra") Kirkaldy (1860-1934) for many years professional to the Royal and Ancient Golf Club. Though he had a distinguished record, he never won an Open Championship. [8I]

KIRKHILL - Formerly known as the Kirk-Heugh this is the site of one of the earliest Celtic churches, founded as early as the sixth century, said to have been moved here from a now vanished island to the north of the long pier known as Lady Craig. It became a collegiate church in 1248-9 and a chapel royal about 1286. The line of provosts continued until 1618. The name was applied in 1975 to the site of the old Fishers School about 150 yards to the west. [3J]

KIRK PLACE - See Golf Place.

L

LADE BRAES - The area between Bridge Street and Cockshaugh Park was developed for housing from 1895. In 1930 a road was formed serving the properties east of Cockshaugh. [5G]

LADE BRAES LANE - This is an ancient thoroughfare from South Street to the lade and is referred to in documents and on maps up to the middle of the nineteenth century as the "Common Close". By 1893 it had become established as "Lade Braes Lane", surviving an attempt by the developers of the backlands of South Street rigs Nos. 116 and 118 from 1848 to call it Madras Place. [5H]

LAMBERTON PLACE - Named 7.11.1979 after William Lamberton, Bishop of St Andrews, 1297-1328, who assisted at the coronation of Robert the Bruce and was an important figure in the War of Independence. During his episcopate the cathedral was consecrated (1318). [9G]

LAMOND DRIVE - Named 12.10.1925 in honour of William Lamond (1866-1928) banker, Buenos Aires, who retired to St Andrews, where he was educated. He served on the Town Council from 1921 and was Provost, 1924-27. [7H]

LANGLANDS ROAD - Named 5.7.1926 after the area of the Priory Acres on which it is built. The area originally consisted of two long contiguous strips totalling about 11 acres and the name is simply descriptive of them. [6I]

LARGO ROAD - On 19.9.1906 it was decided that Largo Road should be the name from Wallace Street to the burgh boundary although the name is obviously descriptive of the ancient road to Largo from St Andrews. Largo = Gaelic leargach = a place of seaward slopes. [8F]

LAWHEAD ROAD - Development began here in 1938 and at the end of that year the burgh boundary was extended to include the street. Three houses were built before the war and development was completed in two phases in the 1950's. On 24.10.1959 it was decided that the street be divided into Lawhead Road East and Lawhead Road West. The street is actually built on part of the lands of Nether Rufflets - Lawhead was that part of the Priory Acres to the south of the Craigtoun road between Law Mill and New Mill. The name refers to the holy ground of the graveyard on the 'hlaw' or Hallow Hill. [6B]

LAWMILL GARDENS - Named 8.9.1969 and refers to the nearby Law Mill or Nether Mill of Balone - a water mill of unknown age, but certainly in existence by the sixteenth century. The Law refers to the Anglo-Saxon word 'hlaw' - the adjacent burial mound known as Hallow Hill. [7A]

LEARMONTH PLACE - Named 18.12.1972 after the family of Learmonth of Dairsie who were virtually hereditary Provosts of St Andrews throughout the sixteenth century. This family interest was perpetuated by the practice of the outgoing town council choosing the new. In the 1590's there arose a successful opposition to the Learmonths and the family disappeared from the burgh and from Dairsie. Lermontov, the Russian poet and novelist, is believed to be descended from this family. [8E]

LEONARD GARDENS - Named 3.9.1973 in memory of Robert Leonard (1889-1973) who was Provost of St Andrews, 1958-61. Born in Liverpool he entered the Customs and excise service as a youth and had over 100 postings before he became customs and excise officer for St Andrews and East Fife in 1936. He retired in 1949 and entered the Town Council in 1950, serving until 1965. He was one of the councillors opposed to the University's plans to expand on the West Burn Lane site in 1957-58. [8B]

LETHAM PLACE - Named 8.9.1969. Letham is a common place name in Scotland, but having various etymologies. The local instance is thought to contain the words laigh+ham - the low lying settlement. [8A]

LINDSAY GARDENS - Named 18.2.1972 in memory of Sir David Lindsay of the Mount (c. 1490-1555), Lord Lyon King of Arms and poet, who studied at St Andrews University. His most famous work is the play "Ane Satyre of the Thrie Estaitis" which has been revived in this century. [8B]

LINKS CRESCENT - Appears in the Valuation Roll in 1919 as the name of the group of houses which had been erected over the previous twenty-five years from Seaton Court Hotel (now Cammo Lodge) at the foot of City Road round to the Atholl Hotel (now part of John Burnet Hall) next Petheram Bridge for which hitherto no official uniform location name had been used. Links is a Scottish word to denote undulating sandy ground, usually beside the sea. [3F]

LINKS, THE - Developed from 1859 taking its name from the adjacent golf links. [2F]

LITTLE CARRON GARDENS - Named 6.7.1994 and taking its name from the lands, on part of which it was built. Little Carron was an ancient property, presumably originally attached to Carron (see Carron Place). It came into the possession of the University in 1852, but was sold in 1901, primarily to provide a site for the Western Cemetery. [7A]

LIVINGSTONE CRESCENT - Named 28.2.1938 at the request of the developers, T Livingstone & Sons, builders. Thomas Livingstone (1875-1957) was on the Town Council at the time, serving as the clerk of works for the first municipal housing scheme. [6H]

LIVINGSTONE PLACE - Named 11.11.1957 after the adjacent Livingstone Crescent and, like it, at the request of the developers, T Livingstone & Sons, builders. [6G]

LOCKHART PLACE - Developed 1851 from designs of 1847, by James Hope (See Hope Street) who named it after his first wife, Charlotte Harriet Jane Lockhart (c. 1828-1858), only daughter of John Gibson Lockhart of Abbotsford, whom he married in 1847. [3G]

LOGIES LANE - Logies Wynd was certainly in existence before the end of the fifteenth century. It derives its name from Thomas Logie, Canon of St Salvators College, who owned property on its west side and who died in 1474. The Wynd was changed to Lane in the renaming of 1843. [4H]

LOUDENS CLOSE - Named after the Louden family who owned this property from about 1820 until 1939. [4H]

18. *The creation of the West Sands Road was an inspired way to dispose of the town's rubbish for over half a century. Another good idea was to use it to create an extension to the University playing fields completed in 1937. The prominent buildings in the background are the Royal and Ancient clubhouse (1853-4 and later additions), the Grand Hotel, now Hamilton Hall (1894) and Rusacks Hotel (1892).*

19. The "traditional" walk along the pier after Sunday service only dates in its present form from after the creation of a University chapel in 1904. The shore buildings in the background housed two taverns; at one end, *The Auld Hoose* and at the other, *The Bell Rock*; in between was a flour mill and a tenement mainly housing fisher families. Behind was the gasworks (first built 1835) whose chimney vies with the ancient monuments for attention.

M

MADRAS PLACE - See Lade Braes Lane.

MAGGIE MURRAYS BRIDGE - Maggie Murray's name first appears attached to what is now Bridge Street - on Ainslie's town plan of 1775 it is called Maggie Murray's Wynd. The bridge is called South Bridge on the 1820 town plan, contrasting with the North Bridge over the Swilcan and Bridge Street is called Well Wynd. It is not until 1854 that a map calls the bridge Maggie Murray's. Accounts have been published this century purporting to identify Maggie Murray and explaining how she paid for the bridge, but they contain several errors of fact, which make them dubious. [5G]

MARINE PLACE - Built by the St Andrews Sea Box Society in 1870. The Sea Box Society was a mutual insurance society set up by the masters, mates and mariners of vessels sailing out of St Andrews. Although sometimes said to have been instituted in 1643, it is certainly older. The Society continued until 1921. [3J]

MARKET STREET - The Narrow Market Gait probably originally existed as a lane giving access to the backlands of the properties in South Street and North Street, but by the sixteenth century it can be identified as a separate street although the Market Place goes back to at least the fourteenth century. It was originally called Mercatgate or Mercatgait becoming Market Street in the course of the eighteenth century. [3H]

MAVIS HAUGH - named 17.12.1985 after the existing house on the site in order to avoid having to re-number the rest of the houses in Hepburn Gardens. An alternative of Montgomery Avenue (see Montgomery Court) was rejected. The original house was erected a year or two before the first World War and was called Howbury. The name was changed to Mavishaugh about 1919 when ownership changed. The name comes from the two Scots words mavis+haugh = the song thrush's flat piece of alluvial land. [7C]

MAYNARD ROAD - Named 4.3.1968 in memory of Maynard the Fleming (fl. c.1140) who is regarded as the first Provost of St Andrews. He is believed also to have produced the first coins struck in the town. [7E]

MELBOURNE PLACE - Named 9.12.1895 being built on ground feued by Alexander Herd, gardener, Otago Cottage, Lade Braes (died 1898), who as a young man went out to the Australian golddiggings and after a moderate success returned to St Andrews. He served as a town councillor and director of the gas company. There was a widespread misapprehension in the town that the development had been called Millburn Place and this name is found even in some official documents for a few years. [5G]

MERCAT WYND - Named 3.12.1980 accepting the suggestion of the developer. 'Mercat' is the old Scottish form of the word 'market' being much closer to the Latin original than the English, which comes from the Latin through French. Mercat Wynd now bears the unofficial name of 'the Mercat Centre'. [3H]

MIDDLESHADE ROAD - Named 22.11.1926 taking its name from that part of the Priory Acres on which it is built. Originally the name - in full, Middleshade of Rathelpie - applied to all the area between Mount Melville Road and the Strathkinness Low Road from the Hepburn Gardens fork out to opposite the junction of the Strathkinness Low and High Roads. Shade = a piece of ground cultivated in one particular direction. [6C]

MILLBURN PLACE - See Melbourne Place.

MOIR CRESCENT - Named 3.9.1973 after Jessie Love Moir (1893-

1987), Provost of St Andrews, 1952-55. Jessie Moir was the daughter of a Glasgow professor and first came to St Andrews as a pupil of St Leonards School. She entered the town council in 1942 and was the first and only woman Provost. [8C]

MONTGOMERY COURT - Named 29.5.1985 in memory of Mrs Frances Montgomery (1894-1972) who had lived here, and given this separate name in order to avoid re-numbering houses in Hepburn Gardens. Mrs Montgomery was a town councillor, 1929-32, and was interested in the administration of association football and sport and was President of the Scottish Polish Society. She also took some of the earliest cine film of St Andrews. [7C]

MORTON CRESCENT - Named 8.9.1969 in honour of James Douglas, 4th Earl of Morton (executed 1581), regent of Scotland, who took a prominent part in public life from the late 1550's and served as regent , 1573-78. His enemies eventually had him tried and found guilty of complicity in the murder of Darnley, an act he actually disapproved of. [8A]

MOUNT MELVILLE ROAD - A short-lived and unofficial name applied by the proprietors of houses built after 1900 west of the Buchanan Gardens fork and recorded on the Ordnance Survey map of 1914. The Town Clerk's view, recorded in 1927, that Hepburn Gardens extended to the burgh boundary, fixed in 1913 opposite Law Mill, prevailed. Mount Melville was the name applied by General Robert Melville to the Craigtoun property he acquired in 1769. The name reverted to Craigtoun when Fife County Council bought the mansion house and grounds in 1952. [6C]

MURRAY PARK - Planned in 1870 and developed 1876-1900 by the Misses Eliza and Mary Ann Murray, joint proprietors of the site which they had inherited from their father, William Murray (died 1869) writer, St Andrews. [3H]

MURRAY PLACE - Planned 1895 and developed from 1896 by the Misses Murray. It survived an attempt in 1900 to rename it Macpherson Street, probably in honour of J. L. Macpherson, treasurer to the Police Commissioners, who also acted as law agent for the Misses Murray. The car park was formed here in 1930. [3H]

MURRAYFIELD ROAD - Named 2.2.1953, the name being the idea of Major J. C. D. Montgomery, the son of Councillor Montgomery (see Montgomery Court), the feudal superior of the site on which it was developed. The name was chosen in tribute to the McKerrow family, his in-laws, who stayed in Murrayfield Road in Edinburgh, but Major Montgomery was also mindful of the name's rugby association and thought it was in any case a good Scots name. [6C]

MUTTOES COURT - Named 4.4.1984 after the adjacent Muttoes Lane and developed on the site of the Cinema House, popularly designated the 'Old' Picture House which functioned 1913-79. [3I]

MUTTOES LANE - This name is sixteenth century in origin from the family Mutto owning property here. It was also known in the sixteenth century as Bakehouse Close (to be distinguished from Bakehouse Wynd). John Mutto/Motto is the best known of the family as he was a lawyer who served as town clerk for fifty years and had property at the Market Street end. His probable near kinsman Andrew Mutto, a baker, had property at the north end of the lane. [3I]

20. *Looking from the top of St Rule's tower (about 1070) across the twin spires at the east end of the cathedral (about 1160 onwards) to the castle (about 1200 onwards). In the foreground are the buildings of the East Infant School which was the name given to the Fisher School after it came under the School Board in 1873. The original building of the Fisher School still survives, obscured by trees in this photo, but the new East Infant School buildings have been replaced by houses (see name index under Kirkhill).*

21. *View at the Step Rock swimming pool in August, 1955 when a week or a fortnight at the sea side was many an urban dweller's dream of a holiday. The swimming pool was developed at the Step Rock in the autumn of 1902. It was shortened and repaired in 1972-73, but disenchantment with outdoor swimming brought its abandonment in a few years.*

N

NELSON STREET - Named 31.7.1912 at the suggestion of Andrew Thom, joiner (1841-1926) who built the first houses here. He chose the name because it was the maiden name of his second wife, Isabella Nelson (1863-1949). [6H]

NEWMILL GARDENS - Named 4.3.1968 taking its name from the New Mill on the Kinness Burn, which functioned from at least 1550 until 1866. The main building of the mill bearing the date 1658 still exists as a dwelling house. [7E]

NORTH CASTLE STREET - In the fifteenth century this was known as Fisher Street (*vicus piscatorum*) and was also occasionally referred to as Sea Street (*vicus maris*). The name Fishergait was in use until the seventeenth century when it was replaced by Castle Wynd. In 1843 the present name was adopted. [3J]

NORTH HAUGH - This was part of the original patrimony of the town and was used at first as common grazing. In the sixteenth century it is referred to as the Cow Marsh (*palus vaccarum*). It was feued or let to individuals from at least the seventeenth century, but in the course of the nineteenth century it was all acquired by the Lairds of Strathtyrum who feued 67 acres of it to the University in 1960 for building. A haugh is a flat piece of alluvial land lying beside a stream and therefore liable to be flooded. [3E]

NORTH STREET - This name is on record before the end of the twelfth century in its Latin form 'vicus borealis'. It appears in the vernacular in the fifteenth century as Northgait which developed into Northgate and in the course of the eighteenth century into North Street. [3H]

O

OLD COURSE - This is the original golfing ground of the burgh although it did not acquire its name until 1895 when a second course 'The New' was laid out. Although it is suggested in some sources that the golf course began by permission of Archbishop Hamilton in 1552 the document referred to does no more than acknowledge that the citizens had enjoyed the right to play golf here and should continue to do so. [2F]

OLD STATION ROAD - St Andrews was first connected to the outside world by railway in 1852 and this road commemorates the original station whose site is now occupied by the Old Course Hotel. The station master's house still remains as the Jigger Inn. After the opening of the new station in 1887 the old continued in use as a goods station and for other railway purposes until 1969. [2F]

p

PARK STREET - No official naming of this street has been found, but the ground was feued by Andrew Berwick, farmer, Rires and the first houses built by William Ness, builder, to designs by David Henry, architect. The warrant for the street was issued and the plans passed in April, 1906. The name seems to mean no more than the street in the field, 'park' in Scots being a piece of enclosed ground. [6H]

PEDDIE BUILDINGS - See Bowling Green Terrace.

THE PENDS - Although long called Pends Road, it was not officially named until 30.3.1964 when the suggestion of the Preservation Trust was accepted. It takes its name from the vaulted gateway which was the principal entrance to the Priory, pend being the Scots word for an arch over an entry. Here there were several arches, hence the plural. The structure is said to have been built as the main ceremonial gateway to the Priory precincts by Prior John Hepburn about 1485, although other opinions place it in either the fourteenth or sixteenth centuries. The road from the Pends to the Sea Yett or Mill Port which is now denoted by the name is certainly very ancient. [4J]

PETHERAM BRIDGE - Dated 1887 this bridge was a necessary part of the diversion of the Guardbridge Road caused by the extension of the St Andrews railway to Anstruther, so completing the 'East Fife coast line' and bringing the station closer to the centre of the town. It took its name from Henry Petheram (1845-95) St Andrews district county road surveyor in succession to his father, who oversaw the work. The last train ran over the bridge 6 January, 1969 and the bridge was shortly afterwards removed, but is to be replaced by a footbridge in 1995. The stretch of road from the bridge to the foot of City Road is often found popularly referred to as Petheram Road. [3F]

PILMOUR COURT - Named 26.11.1986 in order to avoid renumbering the other houses in Pilmour Links of which it forms a part. See Pilmour Links. [3G]

PILMOUR LINKS - Developed from April, 1820 onwards by individuals taking up feus from St Andrews Town Council, who decided in March that year to feu the site for building. It takes its name from Pilmour or Pilmuir Links on the edge of which it was erected. Although other derivations have been suggested, it is likely that this Pilmuir, like the numerous examples of the name elsewhere in Scotland means moor of the fort, the Pil-element being the same as peel. The fort in this case being St Andrews Castle. [3F]

PILMOUR PLACE - Built about 1830-37 by John Buddo. The older name for this road including Pilmour Links (q.v.) was in the sixteenth century Rogergait. The name derived from Cross Roger, a landmark to the north west of St Andrews, very possibly erected by Bishop Roger (1188-1202). [3G]

PIPELAND ROAD - This is an old name for a road going from the South Haugh to the Pyplitland of Balrymonth, a Pyplit being a small piece of land attached to a larger. By the eighteenth century, Pyplitland had become Pipeland and its attachment to Balrymonth lost. The portion between Bowling Green Terrace and Lamond Drive was made into a proper street in 1938 and developed thereafter, the work being interrupted by the war. On 8.5.1939 it was decided that the street named Pipeland Road would run for the whole of the way from Kinnessburn Road to Lamond Drive and it was later continued to Tom Morris Drive. [6H]

PIPELAND WALK - Continues the line of the ancient road to Pipeland from Tom Morris Drive to the burgh boundary and extended as each successive development phase pushed the burgh boundary southwards. Developed from 1970. [8G]

22. *This view from the junction of Priestden Place and Warrack Street shows the prefabricated buildings which were erected as temporary houses in 1946 to help solve the post-war housing problem. They were removed at the end of 1967. The photograph was taken by George Cowie in October, 1956.*

23. *This unusual scene of the Old Course under snow was taken by George Cowie in January, 1960. Distant left is the beach shelter erected in 1926 and demolished in 1989, in spite of local protests, to make more parking space for the golf museum. On the right will be observed the tall chimney of Rusacks Hotel laundry.*

PLAYFAIR TERRACE - Developed 1847-50 and named after Provost Sir Hugh Lyon Playfair (1786-1861), who is on the one hand credited with creating modern St Andrews and on the other with destroying much that was historically interesting of old St Andrews. [3G]

PRIESTDEN PARK - Named 1.7.1948 and like the adjacent Priestden Road taking its name from the land on which it is partly built. [7K]

PRIESTDEN PLACE - Named 1.7.1946 and like the adjacent Priestden Road taking its name from the land on which it is partly built. [7J]

PRIESTDEN ROAD - Named 8.2.1932 after the 28.5 acre park, Priestden, which extended southwards from the Kinness Burn from a point east of the Dempster Brae bridge and on part of which the street is built. A den is a narrow wooded valley with a burn or stream flowing through it, as this was. Why it was particularly associated with a priest or priests has not been recorded. [7K]

PRIORY - The Priory, cloister and grounds were after the Reformation acquired by the Dukes of Lennox who feued them. They were eventually purchased by St Leonards College to repair the Senzie House as a library. This burnt down in November, 1683 "when it was near finished". The college sold the site in 1754 and General Campbell built a house, the Priory House, in about 1804. Lord Bute bought the property in 1893 and set about restoring the Priory buildings in red sandstone, until his early death halted the work. The greater part of the property passed into the hands of the Ministry of Works after the Second World War. Priory House was demolished in 1957 and the site reunited with the Cathedral thereafter. [4J]

PRIORY GARDENS - Named 5.5.1987. The developer suggested "Priory Acres", the traditional name of the whole lands of the Priory on the south and the west of the town (see map 3), but as there was already a house of that name in the town, the new street became Priory Gardens. [7D]

Q

QUEENS GARDENS - Developed 1858-68 and originally called Queen Street in honour of Queen Victoria (1819-1901) who reigned from 1837 until her death. The gardens on the west side were added to the street scheme in 1861. The inhabitants petitioned for years for a change of name from Queen Street to Queens Gardens and eventually usage appears to have won the day against bureaucratic intransigence. [4I]

QUEENS TERRACE - Developed 1867-1901 and originally styled Queen Street Terrace, but as with Queens Gardens usage prevailed. [5I]

R

RADERNIE PLACE - Named 8.9.1969 taking its name from the settlement of Radernie, some five miles south west of St Andrews. There are no references to Radernie earlier than the fifteenth century by which time the name had assumed its present form. Its etymology is probably Gaelic *rath+eireann* = the fortified farmhouse of Ireland (i.e. of the Irishmen). [8A]

RATHELPIE - Although this is not preserved as a street name, it is one of the ancient names of St Andrews and comprehends the lands between Kennedy Gardens, Westerlee, the University Playing fields and both sides of Hepburn Gardens out to Newmill. The ground to the west was called Middleshade of Rathelpie. It is explained as Gaelic *rath+Alpin* = the fort or defended farm house of Alpin, but which of the Alpins, we have no information, though Skene suggests that it was the

Alpin who was slain in 832 and whose son Kenneth succeeded and united the Pictish and Scottish Kingdoms. [5E]

REID GARDENS - Named 3.9.1973 after John Reid (1863-1950) Provost of St Andrews, 1936-1942. A native of Torbrex near Stirling, he came to St Andrews in 1896 to work in the drapery trade and set up his own business ten years later. He served on the Town Council from 1911 to 1942. [9B]

RITCHIE PLACE - An early and quickly superseded name for part of Ellice Place, deriving from James Ritchie, stonemason, who had property here in the 1870's. The name can still be seen carved on the house which he owned. [3H]

ROSE LANE - This is an old entry off South Street which belonged to the Braid family. The name only emerges in the 1840's and was perhaps descriptive of the plants growing there. [4G]

ROSE PARK - The original house was built about 1830 by George Berwick who had a large brewery near the west end of South Street on the north side. The property was later acquired by William Woodcock whose daughter bequeathed it for charitable purposes in fulfilment of which further dwellings were erected in the grounds in the 1970's. [4G]

ROUNDHILL ROAD - Originally named 3.1.1957 and reiterated 9.9.1963, taking its name from the area of the Priory Acres extending to seven acres on which it is partly built. The name is no doubt descriptive. [8I]

RUTHVEN PLACE - Named 18.12.1972 after Patrick Ruthven (1522-66), 3rd Lord Ruthven, who was educated at St Andrews University and played a leading role in the Scottish Reformation, supporting the Lords of the Congregation and having a major role in the murder of Riccio in 1566. He fled to England and died there. [8D]

S

ST LEONARDS ROAD - Warrant was granted for this road on 5.2.1906, but no official naming and no feuing along it took place until 1921. The first feuar's agent was said to have called it Carnegie Gardens, but he must have done so as early as 1912 as it appears on the Ordnance Survey map revised in that year and published in 1914. The University disapproved of the name and decided on St Leonards Road, subject to Town Council approval, "as it was almost in the middle of St Leonards parish". The name was confirmed by the Town Council on both 14.12.1921 and 6.2.1922, two University officials having made independent applications. The name of St Leonard, patron of the sick, is first mentioned in St Andrews in 1248 as the dedication of the Culdee hospital. The church is first mentioned as a parish church in 1413 and in 1512 both church and hospital with the teinds were erected into the college of St Leonards. [5E]

ST MARYS LANE - Takes its name from St Marys College, founded in 1538, on the west side of which it is situated. [4I]

ST MARYS PLACE - Taking its name from St Marys Church (now the Victory Memorial Hall) which was erected in 1839 to provide extra accommodation for the parishioners of the parish church, which use ceased after the reconstruction of the Town Kirk in 1909. The neighbouring houses, some of which predate the church, soon adopted the name. [4G]

ST MARYS STREET - Formed from 1812 onwards by the progressive feuing by St Marys College of that part of the Cunningyard cut off by the new turnpike road to Anstruther. The initial feuing went on to the 1820's, but the street was greatly extended by municipal building in the 1920's. A confusion in the official mind as to what the street is really called has led to its rendering in some documents and maps as

24. *The start of the Scottish Universities cross country race in North Street, February, 1960. In the background on the left can be seen the Cinema House or 'The Old' as the first purpose built picture house in St Andrews was known latterly. It was built in 1913 and closed in December, 1979. Opposite the Cinema House is the hall of the Order of the Eastern Star and another building, both demolished to provide a site for the Crawford Centre and an entrance for the new University Library, which was opened in 1976.*

25. *South Street during the Lammas market in August, 1960. Lammas (= loaf mass) derives its name from the custom of consecrating bread made from the first-ripe corn on the first of August in thanksgiving for the new harvest. The Lammas market in St Andrews now held on the second Monday of the month is the sole survivor of the mediaeval town markets and used to be remarkable up to the First World War for the large numbers of country people and farm servants, who flocked to it seeking new masters. Now it survives as a fun fair and an opportunity for out of town traders.*

St Mary Street. [6K]

ST NICHOLAS STREET - Named 28.6.1926 after St Nicholas farm on the lands of which it was built, overturning a decision on 12.10.1925 to name it Conyngyard Road. The farm took its name from the leper hospital which existed on the land since the early 12th century. Later it became a hospital for the poor under the direction of the Blackfriars and was in use until at least 1583. Some time thereafter the site and its surrounding endowment lands became a farm, coming into University possession in 1865. St Nicholas is the patron saint of sailors and also of children. [6J]

SANDY HERD COURT - Named 9.9.1963 in memory of Alexander (Sandy) Herd (1868-1944), the St Andrean who won the Open Golf Championship in 1902, the first man to do so using the rubber cored ball. [8I]

SANDYHILL COURT - Named 1976, but not minuted probably in the confusion of the changeover of local government from the burgh, which initiated the scheme in 1974 to the District in May, 1975. It takes its name from the adjacent Sandyhill Crescent. This was part of a tripartite gap site development, which saw additional houses (Nos. 19-33) built in Dunolly Place and the two houses called Andrew Thom Place in Kinkell Terrace. [6H]

SANDYHILL CRESCENT - Named 23.10.1939 taking its name from that part of Priory Acres on which it is built. See Sandyhill Road. [6I]

SANDYHILL ROAD - Named 31.8.1936, taking its name from that part of Priory Acres on which it is built, actually East Sandyhill, which extended to 15.211 acres. [7I]

SCOONIEHILL ROAD - Named 13.2.1967 and taking its name from the rise or hill to the south. Early forms of this name consistently render it "Sconin" whose origin is obscure, but which some authors derive from the Gaelic *sgonnan* = a little lump (although this is a term usually applied to a short thick piece of wood). [8G]

SCORES, THE - This is a relatively modern name. The earliest name covering the short part fronting the Castle was Sea Street (*vicus maris*). In the course of the fifteenth century, this became known as Castlegait, while the more westerly section was known as Swallowgait until the eighteenth century. The name Scores derived from Scores Park, i.e. Cliff Park, which lay between the road and the sea and was developed in the course of the nineteenth century (1810-90's). The name is derived from Scots scaur and it in turn comes from the Old Norse *sker* = a short reef or cliff top. [2H]

SHIELDS AVENUE - Named 26.10.1931 in honour of Harry G Shields (1859-1935), managing director of John Shields & Co., linen manufacturers, Perth. A noted artist he lived in the "Swilken", Links Road. He was three years a member of the Town Council from November, 1928 and served as a Dean of Guild, 1929-31. [6J]

SHOOLBRAIDS - Named 9.9.1963 after the area of the Priory Acres extending to about 28 acres through which it passes. Although the name is not unique in Scotland (there is at least another in the Howe of Fife and yet another near Lanark) its etymology is obscure. It is possibly Scots shool = shovel+braid = broad meaning that it was originally divided into very narrow strips. [8H]

SHORE, THE - This part of the road between Shorehead and Balfour Place where it is built up has now mainly storage premises along it although there have at various times in the past been booths, sheds and a few makeshift dwellings here. The name is old and is descriptive of its location. [5K]

SHORE BRIDGE - See Bow Bridge

SHOREHEAD - The earliest building here was in 1770 when the first of a series of granaries, stores and other buildings was erected. In the 1860's some of these were reconstructed by George Bruce (see Bruce Embankment) in a great tenement of housing mainly let to fishermen, which came to be known locally as the Royal George. This was condemned and vacated in the 1930's. In 1964-65 the Royal George was demolished with the buildings alongside except for the former Bell Rock Tavern and flats erected in their place. [4K]

SLOAN STREET - Named 23.1.1922 in honour of Andrew David Sloan (1863-1941), Provost of St Andrews, 1918-24, marking his valuable services in connection with Municipal Housing schemes of which Sloan Street is one of the first local examples. He was minister of Hope Park United Free Church, 1888-1915, and a member of the Town Council 1915-24. With his wife he presented the Child Welfare Centre, in North Street to the town. [5G]

SOUTH BRIDGE STREET - See Bridge Street

SOUTH CASTLE STREET - This was known in the fifteenth century as Rattonraw (street of the rats) with Fisher's Vennel as an alternative. In the sixteenth century it became Huxter Wynd, subsequently Heukster's Wynd (= Wynd of the hucksters or pedlars, retailers of small goods) and so it continued until the renaming of 1843, when it became South Castle Street. [4J]

SOUTHFIELD - Developed in 1879 by Thomas Harris, joiner, on lands which were formerly part of the town common of South Haugh, from which no doubt the name is derived. [5H]

SOUTH HAUGH - Part of the original common lands or patrimony of the burgh. It lay to the east of Bridge Street between the lade and the burn with a small continuation to the south on which Fleming Place, Southfield and Park Street were built. [5H]

SOUTH STREET - This name is on record before the end of the twelfth century in its Latin form *vicus australis* although initially called (c.1144) *vicus burgensium* = street of the burgesses. Southgait appears in the fifteenth century, becoming Southgate before the form South Street is adopted in the eighteenth century. [4H]

SPINKIE CRESCENT - Named 18.12.1972 after the nearby Spinkie Den, which derives its name from the Scots spink which in this part of Scotland denotes the common primrose. [8D]

SPOTTISWOODE GARDENS - Named 25.10.1965 after John Spottiswoode (1565-1639), Archbishop of Glasgow, 1603-15, and Archbishop of St Andrews, 1615-39. His support for the liturgical changes of King Charles precipitated the revolt, which produced the National Covenant in 1638 and the Covenanting Assembly at Glasgow, which declared episcopacy abolished. [7E]

STATION ROAD - The original railway station (1852) was situated where the Old Course Hotel now is and served a branch line from Leuchars, but in 1887 the line round the coast via Crail and Anstruther was completed, involving the building of a new station closer to the centre of the town. After its closure in 1969 the site of the new station was remodelled as a car park and is now occupied mainly by the approach road to the North Haugh car park opened in 1993 and Station Road now serves the Bus Station and taxi rank. [3G]

STRAITON WYND - Named 15.3.1971 after the Protestant martyr David Straiton or Stratoun of Woodstone who was burned at Edinburgh in 1534. Apart from his heretical doctrine, one of the chief parts of his crime was his refusal to pay fish teind to the Prior of St Andrews, throwing back every tenth fish into the sea for the Prior to collect for himself! The name has nothing to do with Straiton in Logie parish, which in fact was only transported to this locality for part of the lands of Cruivie at the beginning of the nineteenth century. The name means "settlement on the [Roman] road". [7G]

26. *St Andrews railway station with the main entrance giving out onto Station Road and pedestrian access from Doubledykes, showing one of the last diesel multiple units on the Fife Coast line, a service which ceased shortly after 10pm on Saturday, 9th September, 1965. British Rail at the same time withdrew the two most popular services to Leuchars and Principal Knox predicted in a letter to The Citizen that the line would close in two years.*

27. *The junction of North Castle Street, North Street and South Castle Street in May, 1983 while a new pavement was being laid. D R Brown's shop in the background was the last of the corner shop groceries in the old town. David Brown took over in 1922 from James Robb whose brother David had had a grocer's shop there since 1856.*

STRATHKINNESS HIGH ROAD - This is an old road from St Andrews via Dairsie Bridge to Cupar, but the name only became possible and meaningful after the construction of the Strathkinness Low Road (q.v.). However in popular usage it continued to be called the Strathkinness Road until the 1930's. One old house existed on this road but it did not become a street until further houses were built. The houses on the south side were developed from 1938 and the houses on the north side were built 1946-48. [5A]

STRATHKINNESS LOW ROAD - The houses which have this name as their address were built in 1938. The road was constructed as a result of the Turnpike Act of 1807 replacing the 'Bishop's Road', which lay further south. [6A]

STRAVITHIE COURT - Named 26.7.1989 for the houses to be built on the site of the Stravithie Dairy at the west end of South Street on the east side. Stravithie is the name of a place some three miles south of St Andrews on the Anstruther Road and is derived from Gaelic *strath+beithean* = strath of the birch trees. [4G]

SWALLOWGAIT - This name probably derives from Scots swail = a hollow and is known from the fifteenth century as applying to that part of the road west of the Swallow Port, which stood at the corner of the Castle yard. Although there are reports of this as a fourth mediaeval street no archaeological remains have been found to support this and it appears to have been bounded on one side by the boundaries of the rigs on the north side of North Street and on the other by grazing land. [3I]

T

THISTLE LANE - Developed off South Street in 1885 for the Misses Thomson and probably named in contrast to the nearby Rose Lane, the thistle being the national badge of Scotland as the rose is of England. [4H]

TOM MORRIS DRIVE - Named 28.5.1951 after the two Tom Morrises, father and son, who are golfing legends. Old Tom (1821-1908) was in charge of the Old Course from 1865-1904 and won the Open Championship (1861,1862,1864 and 1867). His son, Young Tom (1850-74) was also four times Open Champion (1868, 1869, 1870 and 1872). On 18.4.1951 it had been agreed to use the name "Morris Drive" but this was changed at the suggestion of Mr W F Douglas, who thus inaugurated the fashion of double-barrelled street names in St Andrews. [7G]

TOM STEWART LANE - Named 20.1.1975 after the famous club maker Thomas Stewart (1861-1931) who had his 'Pipe Brand' cleek factory in Argyle Street. He was one of the first to produce matched sets of clubs and he invented the hole tin with the concave bottom. This was the last street named by St Andrews Town Council. [8G]

TORFRUNTY - This street name only occurs once in a reference of about 1430 and is probably an early name for what is now the east end of South Street, which lay outside the burgh until the eighteenth century. The only clue is that it contained the property of Archdeacon Thomas Stewart with the property of the priory on the west. This situation certainly occurred here on the south side. The etymology of the name is probably impenetrable but might possibly be Gaelic *torr+froineach* = the bracken mound. [4J]

TRINITY PLACE - Named 18.12.1972 after Holy Trinity Church. The original parish church of St Andrews, dating from about 1144, had been at the east end of the Cathedral. The present building dates from 1412, but was reconstructed in 1798 and again in 1909. [8C]

TULLOCH PLACE - Named 3.9.1973 after William Proctor Alexander Tulloch (1886-1959), the grandson of Principal John Tulloch. He was the manager of a nitrate mine in Chile and retired to St Andrews in 1939. He entered St Andrews Town Council in 1944 and was Provost 1949-52 after which he left the Council. [9B]

U

UNION LANE - This ancient lane ran from North Street to Market Street behind the street frontage properties on the west side of Union Street. It vanished for a time when these properties were mostly cleared under slum clearance schemes before the 1939-45 war, but it still exists though no longer a public thoroughfare. No earlier name is known. [3I]

UNION STREET - This name was introduced about 1830 to replace the earlier name, Foul Waste, which it had borne for at least three hundred years, derived perhaps from the quarry hole and dump, which lay on its west side. The name probably refers to the union of Great Britain and Ireland in 1801 rather than that of England and Scotland in 1707. [3I]

V

VIADUCT WALK - The section of the railway line between St Andrews station and Crail (closed 4.9.1965) within the burgh boundary was acquired in 1968 from British Rail and plans for Viaduct Walk were submitted in 1970. The work was carried out thereafter. The Viaduct from which it takes its name was erected in 1887. [5G]

VICTORIA PLACE - (Largo Road). Plans for the first building at this address were passed on 11.9.1899, but the main part of the development was by Walter and James Anderson, golf club makers, in 1905. It is named after Queen Victoria (1819-1901), who reigned 1837-1901. [5G]

W

WALLACE AVENUE - Named 23.1.1922 after the adjacent Wallace Street. [5G]

WALLACE STREET - Named 12.7.1898 on the motion of Bailie David Henry, architect, along with James Street, but without clue as to reason unless it is after the Scottish national hero, William Wallace (1272?-1305). [5G]

WARDLAW GARDENS - Named 14.1.1901 on the recommendation of the University Court, commemorating Henry Wardlaw who was Bishop of St Andrews, 1403-40. In 1411 he issued the charter founding the University of St Andrews, where teaching had begun in May 1410. He did this because France's withdrawal of allegiance from the antipope, Benedict XIII closed French universities to Scottish scholars. [4F]

28. St Andrews from the North in 1969. The great Victorian terraces of Hope Street, Howard Place and Abbotsford Crescent are one of the most prominent features on the right and show something in their unfinished nature of how the development might indeed have given St Andrews a match for the terraces of Edinburgh New Town as was suggested at the time it was started. The station has not yet been demolished, but the rails to the south have been lifted and the Argyle Street car parks begun. The sharp eyed will notice many other details including the fact that the one way traffic has not yet been introduced.

29. *The prominent feature of this 1971 view of the south west corner of the town is the line of the coast railway (1887-1965) winding its way up the hill to Mount Melville station. The development of the Canongate area has reached Learmonth Place and in the top right Radernie Place and Cairnhill Gardens are just visible.*

WARRACK STREET - Named 27.2.1928 in honour of Frances Jane Warrack (1865-1950) who first came to St Andrews in 1892 as second mistress at St Katharines School. In 1919 she became the first woman town councillor. Although she resigned in 1926 through ill health she returned to serve again from 1932-1934. [7K]

WATSON AVENUE - Named 17.12.1934 in honour of William Watson (1875-1937), burgh engineer of St Andrews, 1900-1937, who had been in charge of laying out the streets for the municipal housing schemes. [6I]

WELL WYND - *See* Bridge Street.

WEST ACRES - Named 19.5.1958 on the suggestion of D.D.R. Owen and simply descriptive of its situation although the University had first proposed "Priory Gardens" and then "Westergard". [5A]

WEST BURN LANE - Previously called West Burn Wynd being the westmost of the two main thoroughfares from South Street down to the Kinness Burn with a cart bridge over the lade. It was renamed West Burn Lane following a decision of the Town Council on 10.11.1843. Its earliest name was Butler's Wynd after the Butlers of Rumgally who owned land on its east side in the fifteenth century. [4I]

WEST PORT MEWS - This unofficial and controversial name was suggested by the developers of the buildings in question, but the District Council on 1.9.1993 instructed that the address should be 205A South Street. [4G]

WEST SANDS ROAD - There was an ancient path out to Eden Point, but it was not until 1914 that it was decided to use the part of the Links next the West Sands as one of the ways in which the town rubbish was disposed of to build a road and reclaim land. In 1918 the site began to be used and remained in use until 1966 when dumping reached Eden Point. Thereafter dumping was transferred to Newton of Nydie. The name is simply descriptive. [1F]

WESTER LANGLANDS - The area of the Priory Acres extending to 72.42 acres on which the University playing fields (except the northernmost part), David Russell Hall and Fife Park are built. The name just denotes an area where the cultivation strips were longer than elsewhere. (cf. Langlands Road, which is built on Easter Langlands.) [5B]

WHITEHILL TERRACE - Developed in 1907 by J. & J. G. Ritchie, builders. The reason for the name has not been determined. [6G]

WINDMILL ROAD - Developed from 1898 taking its name from the town windmill which stood from the sixteenth century until the 1760's on part of the site now occupied by the Bus Station, and it follows the line of the old Windmill Path. [3F]

WINDSOR GARDENS - Named 17.9.1973, overturning a decision on 3.9.1973 to name the street after Provost Cheape, and using the name of the Royal Family. The name from Windsor Castle was assumed by proclamation of King George V on 17 July 1917 in place of Saxe Coburg and Gotha which had been the dynastic title of the Royal Family since the marriage of Albert of Saxe-Coburg-Gotha to Queen Victoria. [9B]

WINRAM PLACE - Named 18.12.1972 after John Winram (c. 1492-1582) sub-prior of St Andrews who became one of the chief Reformers and was Superintendent of Fife and Strathearn from 1561. [8E]

WISHART GARDENS - Named 1.6.1970 after George Wishart (c. 1513-46), the protestant martyr whose death at the stake in front of the castle led to the killing of Cardinal Beaton. His preaching tours in 1544-45 helped popularise the doctrines of the Swiss reformers in Scotland. [8H]

WOODBURN PLACE - Developed from about 1837 by James Gibson, wood merchant, and originally just called Woodburn. The name Woodburn Place was applied first to the row of houses developed within the Woodburn property about 1895 by A. M. N. Miller, boat builder, but now it applies to the road serving the whole complex. The burn is from the St Nicholas burn which flows into the harbour at this point, but whether Gibson named it Woodburn from the trees he planted or from his occupation as a wood merchant can only be speculation. [5K]

WOODBURN TERRACE - Named 25.6.1907 taking its name from the adjacent Woodburn Place. [6K]

30. This photograph of the North Haugh taken by Peter Adamson in September, 1977 shows the following University buildings from the bottom: the Physics building (1965-66), the Mathematics building (1967), the Computing building (1972), the Chemistry/Geography building (1967-68), the Physical Education Centre which is not strictly on the North Haugh (1969) and Andrew Melville Hall (1969).

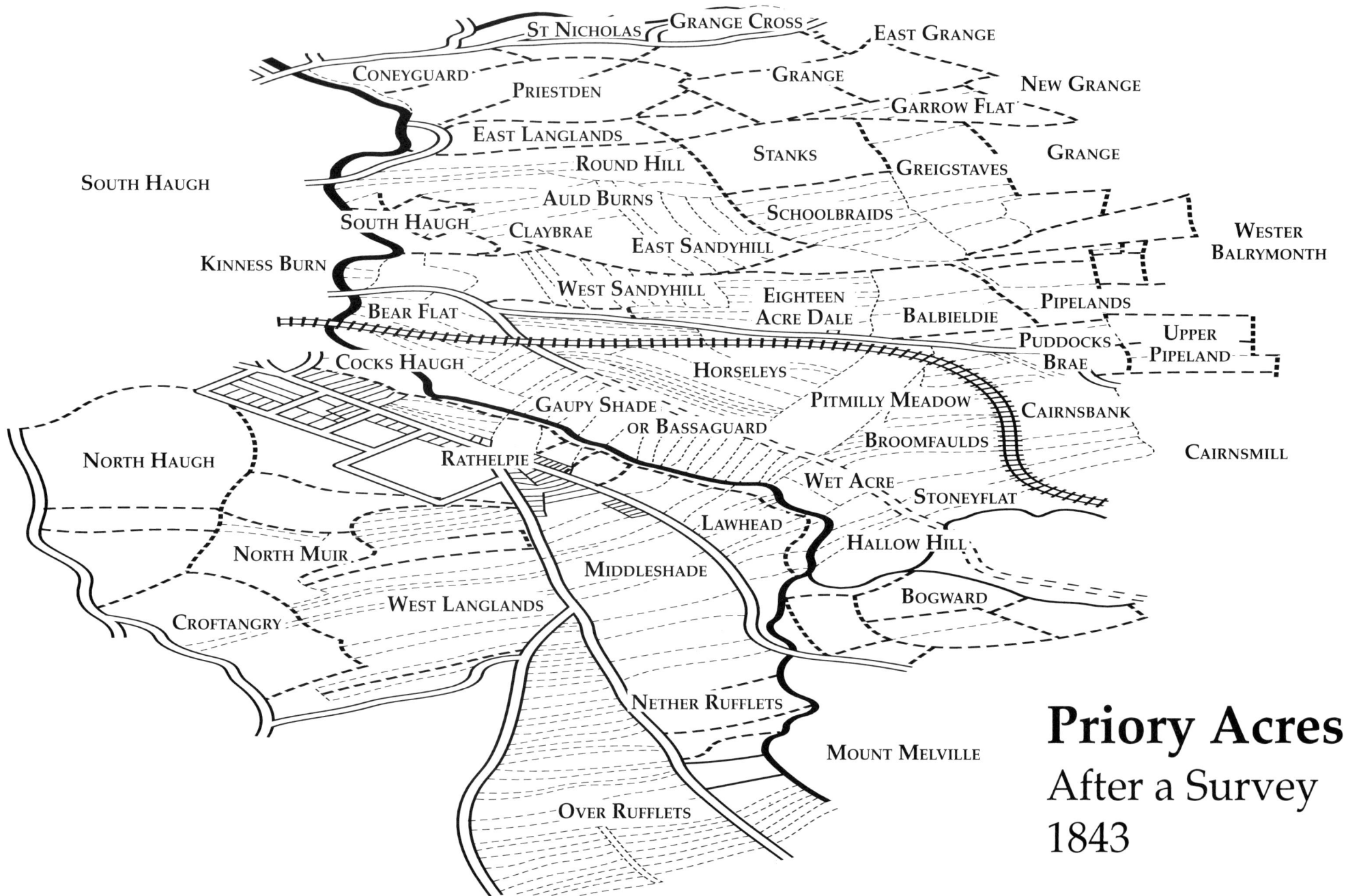

ST NICHOLAS — GRANGE CROSS

EAST GRANGE

CONEYGUARD

GRANGE

NEW GRANGE

PRIESTDEN

GARROW FLAT

EAST LANGLANDS

ROUND HILL

STANKS

GREIGSTAVES

GRANGE

SOUTH HAUGH

AULD BURNS

SCHOOLBRAIDS

SOUTH HAUGH

CLAYBRAE

EAST SANDYHILL

WESTER BALRYMONTH

KINNESS BURN

WEST SANDYHILL

EIGHTEEN ACRE DALE

BALBIELDIE

PIPELANDS

BEAR FLAT

HORSELEYS

PUDDOCKS BRAE

UPPER PIPELAND

COCKS HAUGH

GAUPY SHADE OR BASSAGUARD

PITMILLY MEADOW

CAIRNSBANK

BROOMFAULDS

CAIRNSMILL

NORTH HAUGH

RATHELPIE

WET ACRE

STONEYFLAT

LAWHEAD

HALLOW HILL

NORTH MUIR

MIDDLESHADE

BOGWARD

CROFTANGRY

WEST LANGLANDS

NETHER RUFFLETS

MOUNT MELVILLE

OVER RUFFLETS

Priory Acres
After a Survey
1843